# ILLUSTRATIONS

*Figures*

*Sources of Plates*
Plate 13 is reproduced by gracious permission of Her Majesty the Queen; plate 7 by courtesy of Portsmouth City Libraries; plate 10 by courtesy of the Victory Museum, Portsmouth Dockyard; plate 16 by courtesy of Reyrolle Parsons Ltd.; plate 18 by courtesy of Seaspeed and Castle Studio, Cowes; all the rest by courtesy of the Trustees of the National Maritime Museum.

# SPITHEAD

Other works by Michael Lewis

*England's Sea Officers*
*British Ships and British Seamen*
*The Navy of Britain*
*Ships and Seamen of Britain*
*History of the British Navy*
*A Social History of the Navy 1793–1815*
*The Navy in Transition 1814–64*
*The Spanish Armada*
*Armada Guns*
*Napoleon and His British Captives*
*Ancestors*
*The Hawkins Dynasty*

edited
*The Narrative of Admiral Sir William Dillon,* Vols I and II
*The Commissioned Officers of the Royal Navy,* Vols I, II and III

# SPITHEAD

## *An Informal History*

Michael Lewis

LONDON · GEORGE ALLEN & UNWIN LTD
Ruskin House   Museum Street

Printed in Great Britain
in 11 point Plantin type
by Cox & Wyman Ltd
London, Fakenham and Reading

# CONTENTS

# FOREWORD

My father completed this book on 22 February 1970. On 27 February he died. The text was left partly in typescript and partly in manuscript, and in places was clearly only a first draft. My role, therefore – one that he asked me to assume – has been that of editor, attempting to prepare the book for publication along the lines that I thought he would have followed. I have ventured, here and there, to polish what I felt to be rough, to expand a few passages that seemed to need elucidation, and to remove some repetitions. I can only hope that this treatment has proved beneficial rather than destructive. But I am no naval historian, and I have been enormously helped by three people who have read the typescript through: Robert Sutherland Horne, whose knowledge of Portsmouth and its dockyard is unequalled; Professor Christopher Lloyd, who gave me the benefit of his long experience of naval history; and Richard Ollard, who not only lent me (as he had so often lent my father) his critical and historical talents, but acted, as always, as guide, philosopher and friend.

Although the bulk of the book is thus, in essence, as it was written, there are two substantial additions. The memoir of my father has been provided by Richard Ollard; no one could do it better. Robert Horne has written the final chapter *in toto*; my father had considered something on these lines, but, not being a sailor himself in this sense, he had not even started on it. My gratitude to both of them is thus twofold.

Thanks are also due to Philip Unwin for first suggesting the theme; to Major S. W. Eldridge, Lieutenant-Commander George

Naish, the Rev. J. R. Powell and C. F. C. Ward, for help either to
my father or to me; to Michael Robinson, A. W. H. Pearsall and
other staff of the National Maritime Museum for their guidance
in choosing illustrations; and to all those – acknowledged elsewhere – who have given permission to use their pictures.

M. J. T. LEWIS

# MICHAEL LEWIS

*Spithead* is, sadly, the last work we shall have from the hand of Michael Lewis. Not only was he the foremost naval historian of his day and honoured as such by his fellow practitioners: he was also a writer of marked individuality whose style reflected something of the charm and the humour and the magnanimity and all of the sincerity and unselfconciousness that characterized the man. The originality and the vigour of the fine series of books that began more than thirty years ago with *England's Sea Officers* were as much appreciated by the general public as by scholars and historians. Himself a pupil and a life-long admirer of G. M. Trevelyan, Michael Lewis believed very firmly that history should be readable. He believed too, like Kingsley Amis's hero, that it was not primarily concerned with the price of cows under Edward III, although if such technicalities had to be mastered for the light that might be thrown on more interesting questions his scholarship was never less than thorough and was sometimes superb.

His scholarship and his character indeed so interpenetrated each other that there was no disentangling the two. Uprightness without priggishness, generosity without patronage, largeness of mind without the mistiness that sometimes arises from largeness of heart graced them both. Many of his fellow scholars and many more casual correspondents could multiply evidence of the infinite courtesy with which he answered all letters of inquiry, however elementary or however sophisticated, as though he had nothing better to do with his wide and deep learning than to put it at the service of anyone who inclined to call on it. His own concerns, still more his own ease, naturally came last. Within a few days of his death, when he was struggling against ill-health to finish his own book, he wrote a long and detailed answer to a leading authority who had written to consult him on a point of scholarship. This is but one of the many cases known to the present writer. And this splendid generosity was not tarnished as it sometimes is by an inability to ask or accept the advice or criticism of others or by a disposition to take it, when given, as a matter of course. No man was more appreciative or affectionate in his gratitude. In both relations, giving and receiving, it was the other person, not himself, of whom he thought first.

It is not surprising that such a life should have been enriched at every stage by love and loyalty. The happiness of his own home and family was his joy and his strength in good times and in bad. But there were other attachments; to Wales where so much of his lineage lay, to Uppingham where he and his son went to school, to the officers of the Royal Navy, past and present, in whose service both as educator and historian he had spent his life, and to the host of colleagues to whom he had endeared himself in both capacities. This is to name only the greater streams that fed the broad river of his personality. There were others, higher up, that someone who only knew him in later life might only glimpse or guess. He was not a man that one soon came to the end of.

It would be a disservice to his memory if the affection he inspired were allowed to suggest in the reader's mind the idiotic benevolence of the Cheeryble brothers. He was very far from taking a roseate or unworldly view of the people and things with whom he had to deal. His deep and strong Christianity made him anxious to see the best in people and to make the best out of them, but he felt under no obligation to be bamboozled. Endowed as he was with extraordinary powers of observation and intelligence he saw and understood with a sometimes disconcerting clarity the schemes and manoeuvres of those who because they were acting from less disinterested motives than his own were apt to think that they would easily outwit him. Their confidence was often misplaced. Few men who possessed his tact and adroitness could have resisted as he did the temptation to put them at the service of his own career.

His total lack of vanity and self-importance naturally led vain and self-important men to undervalue him, eager as they always are to catch a reflection of themselves. It was with some difficulty that he was persuaded to accept the Chair at Greenwich in 1934. He had at that time published little in the field of naval history but twenty years teaching at Osborne and Dartmouth had given him experience and opportunity to form his own opinions about education and to distinguish the subject, as his naval and civilian colleagues often failed to do, from training. The General Education course for junior officers at Greenwich over which Michael Lewis presided from its inception in 1946 until his retirement in 1955 was his own creation. He eliminated examinations (because they imposed uniformity of syllabus), reduced lecturing to rational proportions and based the whole course on the seminar and the tutorial. To have done all this anywhere was, at that time, no small feat. To have done so inside the world of service education, apt as it was to be dominated by senior officers with a defensive suspicion of booklearning and by civil servants with a holy terror of what the Treasury might say, required a boldness of vision, an integrity of personality, a patience in threading official labyrinths, an intelligence in anticipating obstruction and a diplomatic persistence of no common order.

Gibbon tells us that the Captain of the Hampshire Grenadiers was not useless to the historian of the Roman Empire. In the same way the first hand experience of negotiation with an entrenched administrative hierarchy was perhaps no less illuminating to the historian of the naval profession and complemented the years of close contact with naval officers at every stage of their careers from cadet to Commander-in-Chief. It is this sympathetic understanding of the naval officer in relation to social ideas and administrative procedures that inspires so much of his most original and important work. No one before him had made sense of the career structure of the navy; no one had analysed the evidence or asked the right questions of it. No one after him can pursue the study without using the channels that he buoyed and lighted.

On a technical aspect of naval history the same could be said of his famous series of articles on Armada Guns which were republished in book form nearly twenty years after they had first appeared in a learned journal. Every subsequent work of scholarship on the Armada campaign has acknowledged the importance of his contribution to the subject. And what a subject! Of all sea-fights none has cast so long a shadow over the history of England or of her sea-power. The Tudor Navy held a special place in Michael Lewis's affections and interests, perhaps because his descent from the Hawkins family quickened his vivid historical apprehension by a direct and personal connection. He was to return to the subject not only in his excellent book *The Spanish Armada* but by way of genealogical themes in *Ancestors* and *The Hawkins Dynasty*. His interest in genealogy, it need hardly be said, was as far removed from snobbery as it was possible to be. It was essentially an embodiment of his understanding of the past, an understanding that owed as much to the sympathy of his historical imagination as it did to the range and accuracy of his remarkable memory. Historical figures were not hostile witnesses to be bullied before a contemporary jury, but people simply. And as such he approached them as he did everyone with charity and courtesy. As a historian and as a man he raised the level of civilization in his own sphere of activities. His long life was happy and useful to a rare degree; and his achievement, like his memory, will not soon be forgotten.

RICHARD OLLARD

# Geographical Prelude

Spithead is that arm of the sea, sheltered from every wind but a southeaster, which lies between Portsmouth and the Isle of Wight. Under part of it lies the Spit Sand, which has given its name to the whole stretch of water. The chart (fig. 1) shows how Spit Sand runs out from Gosport like a sharp-pointed tongue, its upper edge stretching from Fort Blockhouse at the western side of the entrance to Portsmouth Harbour in a roughly south-easterly direction for some two and a half miles; thence returning in a roughly west-nor-westerly direction until it hits the land again at Fort Gilkicker, where the shore itself curves through a right angle to run north-west. Towards the tip of this tongue, Spit Sand Fort rises out of the sea. To the east of the Sand lies the comparatively deep-water channel which leads into Portsmouth Harbour. But even this is markedly shallower than the one which lies south of the tongue, the really deep channel leading to Southampton Water, up which the largest ships in the world can readily proceed. Beyond this channel again the water shoals to the south: but now one is nearing the Isle of Wight.

This is what the modern chart shows. But it was not always so. Once upon a time – a time so long ago that, though young as geology goes, it is yet too old for human history – the Spit Sand was dry ground: and so was most of Spithead, though a considerable fresh-water river ran through the middle of it. If we are asked to give a name to that river, we shall have to admit that we do not know it. It flowed in the days before there were names, and even before there were people to name names. But, for convenience, we

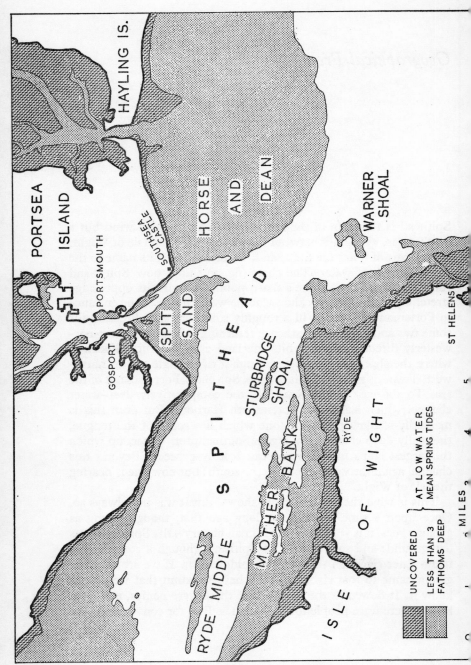

HAYLING IS.

PORTSEA ISLAND

PORTSMOUTH

SOUTHSEA CASTLE

GOSPORT

SPIT SAND

HORSE AND DEAN

WARNER SHOAL

ST HELENS

S P I T H E A D

STURBRIDGE SHOAL

MOTHER BANK

RYDE MIDDLE

RYDE

I S L E   O F   W I G H T

UNCOVERED
LESS THAN 3 FATHOMS DEEP
} AT LOW WATER MEAN SPRING TIDES

MILES

1.   The limits of Spithead

may call it the 'Solent River', for the Solent of today still marks the line of its valley.

Let us look at the geography of southern Hampshire as it was some 12,000 years ago, towards the end of the last Ice Age when the northern parts of Britain were still burdened beneath their load of glaciers. At this time, Wight was not yet an island. The ridge of chalk, which forms its backbone and its highest ground, continued in an unbroken line westwards from the Needles, to join Wight to the Isle of Purbeck near Swanage. At the same time, the level of the sea was markedly lower than it is now. As a result, on the north side of this ridge and parallel to it, there stretched from west to east a wide and shallow valley which contained a river – the Solent River – far bigger than any now existing in the area. It was big because it was fed by many sizable tributaries, all of which are now independent streams, and its most distant sources lay far away, inside the borders of modern Somerset. The first main component of the Solent River was the River Frome. While this now flows down to unite with the Piddle and enter the sea at Poole Harbour, in those days it continued eastwards along a valley bordered on the south by the chalk ridge and on the north by the rising ground behind Bournemouth. As it proceeded, it was joined on the left by the Stour and Avon; by the Lymington and Beaulieu Rivers; by the Test, Itchen and Hamble which had already united to form the ancestor of Southampton Water; and lastly by the smaller streams of the Meon and the Wallington (which now traverses Portsmouth Harbour). On the right bank, as it passed the site of modern Cowes, it collected the only tributary of any size, the Medina, a large stream to be found in so small an island as Wight. Finally the Solent River curled to the right, round the end of the chalk ridge – now marked by Culver Cliff – and eventually mingled its waters with a far mightier river which then ran down the shallow valley now covered by the English Channel. This was a mighty stream indeed, whose headwaters were to be found in central France and which flowed down the wide vale of the Channel, having for its main feeders the Somme and the Seine, as well as all our south-coast rivers.

For in those days not only was the Isle of Wight joined with England, but also England itself was joined with the Continent: where Shakespeare Cliff now confronts Cap Gris Nez across the narrow seas was a continuous range of chalk downs. And, to the north of this barrier, another even greater river meandered down the fenny swamps of the North Sea, having for its tributaries the Rhine, the Meuse and perhaps the Elbe too, not to mention the Thames, Trent and all our eastern rivers, finally emptying into the Arctic Sea abreast of Scotland. In contrast, the great Channel River flowed westward over some three hundred miles in a shallow but ever-widening estuary, to reach the open Atlantic between Ushant and the Lizard.

All this helps to explain how the wide range of animals, whose bones are still to be found all over England, came to get there – from the Ice Ages the bison, the woolly rhinoceros and the bear; from the warmer intervals the elephant, the hippopotamus and the sabre-toothed tiger. They had not had to swim across: they had simply walked. And so had palaeolithic man, who passed back and forth over the land-bridge between us and Europe, to leave his flint implements in the gravel beds which had been washed down by the rivers on whose banks he eked out a hard and precarious existence.

Using our imagination, we can see from the sketch map (fig. 2) roughly what prehistoric Hampshire looked like. From the high chalk backbone of Wight, gazing westwards, a man would see the ridge that was his vantage point stretching away in a nearly straight line into the dimmest distance, with the Solent River meandering towards him below its northern slopes. As he turned his eyes round to the north, the observer would see this valley more clearly: wide and low-lying, with lesser tributaries running down to join it along reed-fringed beds over rather flat land. Behind these streams he could spot the higher ground of modern Hampshire with, prominent to the north-east, the line of the Portsdown Hills behind what is now Portsmouth Harbour but which was then indistinguishable from the rest of the landscape. The country, in the main, would be clothed in scrubby grassland and studded with birch and hazel, the prelude to the thick forests that were to spring

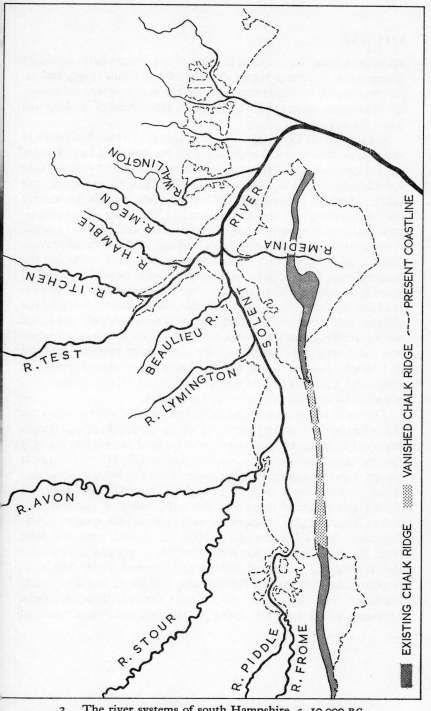

R. WALLINGTON

R. MEON

R. HAMBLE

R. ITCHEN

R. TEST

BEAULIEU R.

R. LYMINGTON

R. AVON

RIVER

R. MEDINA

SOLENT

R. STOUR

R. PIDDLE

R. FROME

EXISTING CHALK RIDGE

VANISHED CHALK RIDGE

PRESENT COASTLINE

2.   The river systems of south Hampshire, *c.* 10,000 BC

up in later ages. To the east, the line of the Solent River could be discerned as it swung round the end of the chalk ridge, and be followed down into the great plain on the south, where occasional glints of wider water might be caught at some bend of the Channel River estuary.

But the Solent River vanished long ago, for the sea has swept in upon it, drowning it in something over one hundred feet of water at its deepest. There were two reasons for this drastic change. One – the lesser one – is that the whole of the land mass gradually sank below its earlier level, a process still at work, though fortunately very slowly, in south-east England today. The other and predominant reason is that with the decline of the last Ice Age, the glaciers retreated by the simple process of melting in the ever-improving climate. In doing so, they released vast quantities of water and the sea level rose. Even today, unbelievable masses of water are locked up in those last bastions of the Ice Age, Antarctica and the Greenland ice-cap, and were there to be another general warming of the climate, this water would be set free, with a catastrophic rise in the sea level throughout the world. So it was in earlier days. Not only was the North Sea formed and the chalk ridge between England and France broken down, but the Great River was drowned to create the Channel, its tributary, the Solent River, disappeared beneath the sea, and Wight became an island.

The rib of chalk from Wight to Purbeck was nibbled away on the north by the river, and by the rising sea on the south, until a breach occurred and the rest was worn away by tidal action, leaving only the truncated stumps of the Needles and of Old Harry Point near Swanage to point to its former course. Thus the Frome, Stour and Avon now debouch straight into the Channel, while only the Solent and Spithead remain to mark the valley of the erstwhile Solent River. England became an island somewhere around 7,000-6,000 BC; Wight became one at about the same time or a little later. As the irresistible sea level climbed, it spread out to drown the lower-lying tributary valleys and created Poole Harbour, Southampton Water, and Portsmouth, Langstone and Chichester Harbours. Had it climbed only a little further, those last three harbours would not exist today, for though the Wight shore of

Spithead rises steeply around Ryde, the mainland shore from Gosport through Portsea, Hayling and Thorney Islands is very low-lying. Eastward again, Selsey has seen many vicissitudes, with its shingle banks being alternately built up and eroded by the currents. The Owers Bank off Selsey Bill was dry land in historical times.

So much for the land now visible: what of those parts beneath the water? West of Wight, the scouring tides of millennia have completely altered the drowned contours of the land. In the narrows, in spite of natural scouring and silting and artificial dredging, the beds and banks of the old rivers are still there, more or less, though they are now covered, even at low tide, to depths that range from more than a hundred feet to as little as one or two feet. If we look at the modern chart we can still see, roughly, where the rivers ran, and what in the old days was dry land. We shall find, for instance, that the Spit Sand is nowhere covered at low tide by more than three fathoms or eighteen feet of water, which near the Gosport shore shrinks to nothing. And we shall still find that on the site of the old rivers the depth of water increases rapidly. Along the east of Spit Sand, the old bed of the River Wallington, where it emerged to join the Solent River before it was reduced to a short stream by the creation of the harbour, now forms the channel to Portsmouth itself. It is nowhere less than 5 fathoms (30 feet) deep at high tide, and right under Fort Blockhouse at the harbour entrance there is $11\frac{1}{2}$ fathoms (69 feet). The main through channel to Southampton, where it follows the bed of the Solent River, always has at least $11\frac{1}{2}$ fathoms (69 feet) at high tide, though Southampton Water itself has a minimum depth of $9\frac{1}{2}$ fathoms (57 feet). At the man-of-war anchorage at the heart of Spithead, the depth ranges from $15\frac{1}{2}$ to $19\frac{1}{2}$ fathoms (93 to 117 feet) at high water. The Solent west of Cowes tends on the whole to be shallower than Spithead, no doubt because it is higher up the old valley and above the point where the river was boosted by the tributaries emerging from the Southampton direction. As a result, the largest modern ships always proceed out into the Channel via Spithead and not via the Needles.

Yet of course as viewed from, say, Ryde Pier, the whole spread

23

of Spithead is a flat expanse of water, right up to the Portsmouth and Gosport shores. To look at, in fact, it might be all of a uniform depth, though a moment's reflection will tell us that this cannot be so – else, of what use are the innumerable buoys, towers and channel marks which tell each ship where to find the depth of water that she requires?

For the watcher on Wight Downs, what a contrast between then and now! For now there is salt water all around. You know it, though doubtless there are very few places from which you can actually see water in every direction. It is, of course, as the observer looks north over Spithead and the Solent that the difference becomes most marked. For this is not only sea where before it was dry land, but also it is a highly occupied stretch of sea, with plenty taking place on it to catch the eye; the yachts at or off Cowes, the great liners bound to or from Southampton, together with freighters of all sizes and shapes, and under all sorts of national flags. Then, with luck, on the broad bosom of Spithead itself, the observer may descry the sober grey forms of warships, again of all shapes and sizes. And, threading through it all, is an ever-moving kaleidoscopic procession of smaller vessels carrying the traffic, both goods and passenger, as it shuttles from the mainland to the island and back – ordinary tramps, car ferries, pleasure boats, even hovercraft. For now the island is one of the great playgrounds of Britain, of a people who still love islands. And here is an island, in itself beautiful and largely unspoilt, yet within easy reach of the Metropolis and the overcrowded suburbs that ring it about. Moreover, now that sartorial colour has once again invaded man's (and still more woman's) holiday attire, what a sight it is in the summer months and on sunny days, with people in their thousands and ten thousands plying constantly between Portsmouth and Ryde – right across Spithead – or between Southampton and Cowes – right across the Solent – sailing, or half-flying, over the sparkling sun-flecked waters which in summer are seldom rough.

Half these people and more are steaming, sailing or skimming across Spithead. Yet perhaps, as they do so, they have neither the time nor the inclination to consider the history which lies on or under it. Let them but think a moment, though, and they will realize that a stretch of sea like this, lying as it does just next door to the greatest naval harbour in the country – and for long in the world – simply must be redolent of history; for no naval craft has yet been able to enter or to leave Portsmouth without traversing it.

The principal aim, then, of this book is to disentangle as many strands of its history as possible, and lay them out for the information – and if possible the interest – of those who cross it, or who, at some future day, may do so.

It remains important to inform the reader precisely where Spithead is. The reader knows? But does he? It is open to doubt. The present author, when he decided to write on this subject, thought it well to discover exactly where it really was – *exactly*; he already knew *roughly*. And this took a surprising amount of doing. He inquired of local authorities such as harbourmasters, and he inquired of local users – distinguished yachtsmen and the humbler boatmen. But none of them could tell him Spithead's exact bounds. Indeed, one senior Admiralty official who lived on the very spot was so bothered by the question that he was reduced to pointing; replying with an airy wave of his hand, 'There, damn it – just outside my blasted window!'

Actually, as this painstaking author ultimately discovered, he was wrong, just. The answer appears in *The Solent Chartbook* of the 1890s, where we learn that Spithead

> may be defined as bounded on the north by the Spit Sand, on the east by the Horse and Dean, on the south by the Sturbridge shoal and Motherbank and on the west by Ryde Middle.

Figure 1 shows its exact limits. Notice that, by this definition, our Admiralty friend was out, if only by a little. He forgot, or perhaps did not know, that as he sat in his sea-blown office, the Spit Sand still separated him from Spithead proper. But these are minutiae.

Strictly as a geographical expression, then, Spithead is a stretch of water about five miles long from east to west and a bare two miles from north to south. But in this book it is proposed to take a more liberal view of this famous anchorage. We shall take cognizance of things which occurred anywhere between the Owers Bank off Selsey and the entrance to Southampton Water, and, north to south, anything from Portsmouth itself to the Isle of Wight; and to be on the safe side, we shall include happenings in St Helens Road, which lies off the extreme eastern point of the island, because that was always the starting and finishing point for naval ships outward or inward bound from or to Spithead.

Yet – blow it all – everyone, be he navy man, yachtsman, or just passing sightseer out to enjoy himself, knows in his heart where Spithead is. So let us say no more about it, but conclude with an extract from the delicate pen of the incomparable Jane Austen.

She is writing *Mansfield Park*, and her heroine, Fanny Price, is standing on the ramparts overlooking Spithead, with her sister Susan and her hated lover Mr Crawford. And in spite of the company, what a peach of a day it was.

> The day was uncommonly lovely. It was really March, but it was April in its mild air, brisk soft wind, and bright sun, occasionally clouded for a minute; and everything looked so beautiful under the influence of such a sky; the effects of the shadows pursuing each other on the ships at Spithead and the island beyond, with the ever-varying hues of the sea, now at high water, dancing in its glee and dashing against the ramparts with so fine a sound, produced altogether such a combination of charms for Fanny, as made her gradually almost careless of the circumstances under which she felt them.

This was written one hundred and fifty years ago by one who knew the scene intimately and who loved what she knew. But Spithead is still like that, whenever the sun shines and the fresh breeze blows.

*Chapter I*

# SPITHEAD BEFORE THE RISE OF PORTSMOUTH

That stretch of sea now known as Spithead has been in existence, of course, far longer than the town which lies to the north of it. Yet – until Portsmouth made its appearance as a town and as a naval base rather than as a mere hamlet – this particular sheet of water had comparatively little significance, except as part of a deep channel which led from the open sea to the heart of England. So, really, the history of Spithead may be said properly to have begun only when Portsmouth had been founded properly. Yet it is hardly true to say that, till that moment, it *had* no history. Spithead was there. It must have had some history, not, as it were, in its own right, but as a part of a larger whole; as a part of the way up Southampton Water or – before Southampton itself ever existed – as an integral part of the sea-road into England, and a piece of that stretch of water which made Wight an island. So this part of the story must be considered first. But, until the arrival of Portsmouth, it shall be told briefly, for, traditionally, Spithead without its Portsmouth is rather like Hamlet without its Prince.

Portsmouth, as we shall see, was in existence under that name in 891, probably in the form of a small fishing hamlet. It is not mentioned in the Domesday Survey of 1086, though what later became integral parts of it were there under other names. This is curious. There is some cause to think that Henry I may have given Portsmouth its first Charter in 1106, but this is not a certainty. This Charter cannot at present be found, but it is certain that by 1194 the town was considered big enough and rich enough to be granted a Charter at the hands of Richard Coeur de Lion, who had already been using the facilities of its harbour for the fitting out of his ships for the great Crusade.

Now for a brief summary of Spithead's history before that. It is most unlikely that the inundation of the area already described caught our palaeolithic men napping. Yet they did disappear in due course, driven out by a succession of peoples of higher culture, who commanded better weapons of war and superior instruments of agriculture. There were many such invasions, which cannot be followed in detail here. All that can be done is to record some of the later arrivals.

In late prehistoric times – the last few centuries before Christ – the Hampshire coast began to play a role it has maintained to a greater or lesser degree ever since; that of serving as a convenient terminus for cross-channel commerce from north-west France, or Gaul as it then was. The shorter route across the Straits of Dover indeed remained in constant and heavy use, but in the absence of easy land transport on either side, the longer crossing from Normandy and even Brittany to Hampshire saw much coming and going, as witness the many finds on the English side of late Iron Age imports, notably the hoard of Gaulish coins from Portsmouth itself. Along this route, from about 150 BC, came several waves of raiders from Gaul who penetrated inland, ultimately settled, and disseminated their own culture. Much of Hampshire and the western end of Sussex was thus populated by people known as the Atrebates, an offshoot of a tribe of the same name from the Arras district.

The middle of the last century before Christ saw the first movement of Roman might in Britain's direction. Julius Caesar conquered Gaul and made two brief forays to Britain (55 and 54 BC), which were designed partly for reconnaissance and partly, by overawing the British rulers, to prevent them from lending aid to their Gaulish kinsmen. Caesar, landing in Kent, did not reach as far as Hampshire. But soon after his visits, more mass migrations took place from Gaul. About 50 BC some of the Belgae – their name is preserved in the modern Belgium – crossed the Channel and established themselves in southern Hampshire, with their centre at Winchester.

28

These were the people – far from uncivilized, adept in the use of iron, and in close commercial contact with Roman Gaul – who lived in our area when the Romans invaded Britain in force in AD 43. Again, the conquerors landed in Kent and fanned out north, north-west and west across the country. Among their early diplomatic successes was a treaty with Cogidumnus, king of the southern Atrebates at Chichester, whose splendid palace at Fishbourne, just west of that city, was recently excavated and can now be visited. His territory, which thereafter enjoyed the Latin name of Regnum, the Kingdom, proved invaluable as a springboard for the Roman advance along the south coast. The Commander of this prong of the army was the future emperor Vespasian who, before carrying the offensive further west, conquered southern Hampshire and the Isle of Wight. Wight is but the Saxon form of the Roman name for it, Vectis, which itself derives from a Celtic word meaning, it has been said, 'fork' or 'turning', after the great bend in the Solent opposite Southampton Water.

The land once conquered, the process of Romanization began. It was not marked by mass slaughter or depopulation, but by a tolerant administration established over the local inhabitants, encouraging them to adopt the Roman way of life. A new town sprang up on the site of the Belgae's old capital: Venta Belgarum, now Winchester. Another sizeable settlement, Clausentum, appeared at Bitterne just across the Itchen from Southampton, where it served as perhaps the main port of the south coast. According to the geographer Ptolemy there was, somewhere on the Hampshire shore, a harbour called Portus Magnus, the Great Port; and enthusiastic Portsmuthians have claimed it as Portsmouth Harbour. Maybe: it may equally have been Southampton Water. Villas were built, the often comfortable country houses that served as the centres of farming estates. Their owners, far from being the tyrannical and pleasure-seeking military overlords to whom popular imagination ascribes them, were more often wealthy Romanized Britons. In the mellow climate of the Isle of Wight no less than seven villas have been discovered, the best known and most lavish being that at Brading; there were others besides, in the hills behind Portsmouth. For communications inland, a road was engineered from Chichester westwards, between the Portsdown hills and Portsmouth Harbour, to Bitterne; from there it ran north via Winchester to Silchester (Calleva), the capital of the Atrebates, at the extreme northern boundary of the county.

After the initial conquest, no military establishment at all was kept in the district for a good two centuries. The waters of Spithead were undoubtedly furrowed by many ships, both ferries to the Isle of Wight and merchant vessels trading in and out of Southampton Water and perhaps Portsmouth Harbour. There were no doubt visits from the Classis Britannica, the British fleet, that served in these parts as coastal police and customs, rather than as a truly military force. Little, in fact, happened to disturb the peace of the district until in the late third century a new menace appeared. Bands of marauding Saxons began to sail down the North Sea from their homes in north-western Europe and to land, intent on pillage, on the south and east coasts of Britain.

The Romans' answer was to increase the size of the Channel fleet and to intercept the raiders before they could land, or to pick them up, laden with booty, on their homeward journey. A string of heavily-fortified bases for the fleet to operate from was established around the coast from Norfolk to Hampshire, the westernmost member of this series of 'forts of the Saxon shore' being Portchester Castle at the inland end of Portsmouth Harbour. Its impressive walls, with a Norman keep tucked into one corner, remain among the most upstanding of Roman structures in the country. Another possible fort of this kind exists at Carisbrooke on the River Medina in the Isle of Wight, where Roman masonry is embedded in the medieval castle. So here at length Spithead came into its own as the scene of real naval activity, for no fleet could get to Portchester without passing through it. During the latter part of the Roman period it must have seen many a fully-armed and manned Roman galley.

This was certainly the case in AD 296. Nine years before, Carausius, Admiral of the Channel Fleet, had been accused of striking bargains with the pirates, and to avoid trial he had set himself up as self-styled Emperor of Britain. After six years he was assassinated by his minister Allectus, who, anticipating the inevitable attempt by the central empire to recover Britain, set his ships cruising off the Isle of Wight while he himself watched the Kentish coast. Sure enough, before long the Caesar Constantius launched an invasion from Gaul. It had two prongs. Constantius himself made a straightforward landing in Kent, and sent his lieutenant Asclepiodotus to enter Britain via the Solent and to fall on Allectus's rear. This western force made contact with the rebel fleet as it was cruising off Wight, but before there could be any fighting a dense fog came down which completely blinded the defenders, allowing Asclepiodotus to creep past them and enter the Solent. Having set out from the Seine, he probably entered the enclosed waters from the east; and, if so, he must certainly have reached Spithead. But whether he disembarked in Portsmouth Harbour or went on up the Solent and landed somewhere in Southampton Water we do not know. Anyway, his mission was a complete success. Allectus, reeling before Constantius, retreated back as far, perhaps, as Woolmer near Aldershot, where he ran into Asclepiodotus and was obliterated.

Thus the Empire regained Britain whence, in due course, Constantius's son, Constantine the Great, beginning his career in this country, issued forth to control the world and accept the Christian faith.

With the removal in the early fifth century of all Roman troops from Britain, to meet the mounting pressure of barbarian attacks on other more important frontiers, our coasts were left open to the ravages of the Saxons. These fierce and relatively uncivilized tribes, untouched by Christianity or the influence of Rome, came at first for plunder but later to settle in a land more fertile than their own and now lying at their mercy. Indeed, in some cases Saxon bands were positively invited in by those in authority, simply to act as mercenary soldiers and to keep out their more ravenous brethren.

The precise course of the Saxon settlements in Hampshire can hardly now be disentangled. The earliest written evidence we have was in fact compiled so long after the event that we can by no means necessarily take it as sure fact. Some of it can be accepted with safety: the statement, for example, about the inhabitants of the Isle of Wight by the Venerable Bede, who wrote in 731. The people, he says, of most of the kingdoms existing in England in his day were descended from two of the three invading tribes, the Angles and the Saxons. But from the third and smallest, the Jutes, 'are descended the people of Kent and the Isle of Wight, and those in the province of Wessex opposite the Isle of Wight are called Jutes to this day'. Archaeology and the study of place-names agrees that there was a cultural link between the people of south Hampshire and those of Kent. These Jutes began to settle in perhaps the early sixth century, and seem to have remained as a minor but independent kingdom until they became pawns in the power game being played by their mightier neighbours. In 661 Wulfheare of Mercia captured the Isle of Wight and a stretch of the mainland opposite, and gave them to the South Saxons of Sussex; and in 686 Caedwalla of Wessex took the island once more and killed off the remnants of its Jutish dynasty. Thenceforward the area became a part of Wessex.

Archaeological finds strongly suggest that the great kingdom of Wessex was originally built up by Saxons moving up the Thames valley, not striking inland from the south coast. But the Anglo-Saxon Chronicle, whose oldest manuscript dates from the late ninth century, contains several entries that contradict this. Under the year 495 it introduces us to a character who became very important in tradition, even if his historical activities are dubious. Cerdic was counted as the founder of the royal house of Wessex, the forebear of King Alfred, and to this day heralds place him at the head of the Queen's ancestors.

This year there came into Britain two leaders, Cerdic and Cynric his son, with five ships, at a place called Cerdices-ora [possibly Totton at the head of Southampton Water]. And they fought with the Welsh [the Celtic Britons] the same day.

The Chronicle goes on to recount Cerdic and Cynric's later victories inland; the foundation of the kingdom of Wessex; how they took the Isle of Wight and slew many men in Wihtgaras-byrg

1. The Battle of Spithead, 1545. The English fleet occupies Spithead; to the left, the French fleet clusters around St Helens. Portsmouth is at the bottom right and Southsea Castle at left centre. Above the castle, the *Mary Rose* is sinking

2. Vernon's fleet lying in Spithead, 1741, viewed from Ports Down. Portchester Castle is at the bottom right, Portsmouth in the centre, Southsea Castle at left centre, and the Isle of Wight in the background

3. Portsmouth from Southsea Common, 1765. Between Southsea Castle (extreme left) and the Harbour entrance (left centre) are Haslar Hospital and Fort Blockhouse

(possibly Carisbrooke); and how, on Cerdic's death in 534, the island was handed over to his nephews Stuf and Wihtgar.

How much reliance can we place in this account? It is at odds with all the other evidence, literary and archaeological, and raises an additional enigma in that Cerdic's name is not Saxon at all, but Celtic. To part of the problem a reasonable and human answer can be given. The Chronicle shows strong signs of having been compiled in Wessex, for the West Saxon royal family; and it may well be that the story of Cerdic was invented, or at least embroidered, to add colour to Wessex's claim to the Jutish district of Hampshire, and to provide a respectable ancestry for the West Saxon kings. Who would not prefer to trace his lineage back to a valiant sea-lord who fought his way inland against heavy odds to found a mighty kingdom, rather than to an anonymous batch of doubtless ragged bandits who straggled slowly up the Thames valley and ultimately acquired their territory by intermarriage? Cerdic may have existed; he may possibly have founded Wessex; but it is doubtful whether he did all that is said of him, or even (with his Celtic name) whether he came by sea at all.

Yet another query is raised by those gentlemen Stuf and Wihtgar, who were endowed with the Isle of Wight. Stuf may be a genuine historical figure, but Wihtgar smacks of that old habit of inventing allegedly historical characters and using their names to explain placenames. Wihtgaras-byrg does not mean 'the fort of Wihtgar', but 'the fort of the men of Wight (Wihtwara or Wihtgara)'. Of just the same kind is the Chronicle's entry for 501:

This year Port and his two sons Bieda and Maegla came to Britain with two ships, at a place called Portsmouth (Portesmutha). They soon landed, and slew on the spot a young Briton of very high rank.

We can be quite sure that Port was dreamt up to account for the name of Portsmouth. The main interest of this entry, in fact, is that it is the earliest mention we have of Portsmouth as a place. We need not accept that it was there in 501; still less is there any trace of Roman occupation on the site. We can only be certain that it

c

existed by 891, when our oldest copy of the Chronicle was compiled. Indeed, there is little room for doubt that the obvious derivation of the word is the right one, the mouth of the port, the mouth of the great harbour. That harbour *may* have been the Portus Magnus of the Romans, and Portchester *may* have been called Portus Adurni. And very shortly after Portsmouth first appears as a place name, the connected names of Portchester, Portsdown and Portsea all appear too. It is a reflection of the growing importance of that great natural port in Saxon times, and Port as a man can decently be consigned to oblivion.

What of Spithead itself among all these historical niceties? Throughout the Saxon period it is never mentioned as such, but it saw some stirring events as well as plenty of ordinary ones. Of the invaders, the Jutes definitely, the West Saxons much less probably, sailed through it as they ranged westwards along the coast. It no doubt played its part in carrying the fleets involved in Wight's violent if nebulous history. By the eighth century it provided a route for more peaceful traders, bringing in pottery from the Rhineland and wine from the Seine to the new port of Hamwih or Hamtune, the forerunner of Southampton. It saw the humble and (to us) ill-defined rise of the settlement that was ultimately to dominate it, Portsmouth itself. Finally, it was ploughed once more by the fleets of a new and terrible scourge.

In 787 a small fleet of three hitherto unknown craft raided the south coast of Wessex, disappearing again over the horizon before anyone could do anything about it. These were the dread Viking ships, the first of the Norsemen's 'drakars'; and the people who manned them, known in England by the generic name of Danes, were only doing what, some three centuries before, the Saxons themselves had done. Since that day, however, the Saxons had for the most part left the sea and become farmers, so that they now found it difficult to defend themselves. But they were not such easy prey as their original opponents – the Celtic Britons – had been, who, softened by long centuries of the Pax Romana, had been unable to defend themselves on either sea or land. Whatever else they were, the Saxons proved themselves magnificent soldiers in the defence of what they had long come to regard as their homes.

But the Danes persisted, following the example of the Saxons before them. At first they came merely to plunder, attacking in particular the rich monasteries which lay scattered over the whole face of Britain, representing the piety of the long-since converted Saxons. But the Danes had not been converted, and were more barbarous and, if possible, more cruel than the Saxons. And very soon, like them, they came to stay, if they could but gain a foothold. The contest that followed was very equal, the English prevailing as a rule on land, because they usually outnumbered the ship-borne Danes: who, however, were much superior at sea and able constantly to exploit the weapon of surprise, because they simply came up over the horizon at will and launched their attack where and when they liked.

In 833 they came in strength to Charmouth near Lyme Regis, challenging the power of Wessex, and four years later they appeared in force at Spithead. Sweeping up the Solent, they attacked Southampton, then a small but rising port, but were driven off by the local ealdorman Wulfheard. Now, however, the Danes had glimpsed the promised land, and they renewed their efforts to gain a more permanent foothold. They came very near success in 860, when they tried again, both by sea and by land – by sea over Spithead and by land via Portchester. This time they succeeded in taking Southampton and advancing up the Itchen to Winchester, which in turn they took and sacked. Indeed, they were only prevented from going further inland by reinforcements coming down from Berkshire.

But by now we have reached the reign of the great King Alfred who, among many other things, saw the necessity of meeting the Danes on their own element, so creating what must be known as the first English Navy. It was the coming of this new 'arm' to the people of this island which was ultimately to have an immense effect on the quiet waters of the Solent. For here, ready to hand, was an abundance of sheltered anchorages. And the one which gradually gained pride of place of them all was Spithead. But not in King Alfred's day. Although it doubtless saw on many occasions the passage of that great king's ships, there was nothing yet in the immediate hinterland of Spithead that really stood in need of permanent defence.

The immediate result of the near-hundred years' war was a compromise. In 878, after Alfred had suffered a resounding reverse, followed by an even more resounding victory, English and Danes got together at Wedmore, and partitioned the country. Guthrum the Dane, in return for his conversion to Christianity, was to hold the north and east of the island, Alfred retaining the rich south and west. The dividing line for the most part ran down the line of the old Roman road of Watling Street, which is approximately the line now followed by the A5.

After that things were temporarily more peaceful in South Hampshire, which was now a long way on the Saxon side of the line. Guthrum on the whole kept to the terms of the treaty, but in due course both he and Alfred disappeared from the scene. In the time of the feeble Ethelred the Unready the Danes resumed their assaults on the south, and many times in the thirty years after 980 they ravaged Hampshire and the Isle of Wight. A typical entry in the Chronicle reads, '998. At another time they established themselves in Wight, and got their food the while from Hampshire and Sussex.' The economic effect of these devastations is shown by the fact that nearly a hundred years later, at many places on the Hampshire coast, taxes were still being remitted because of the damage suffered.

At last the Danes acquired all England. It was, however, Canute, the greatest and best of all the Danes, who now ruled the country, favouring the English rather than his own people. It was only after he and his immediate heirs had gone, and when the old Royal House of Wessex had come into its own again, that another enemy arose who threw all into the melting-pot once more. It was now that the Normans, another branch of the Norse family (but now so long resident across the Channel in Normandy that they had become a highly civilized people), appeared on the scene: and it was Edward the Confessor, the last of the old English dynasty, who allowed himself to fall under the thumb of the greatest Norman of them all – William, known to us as the Conqueror. This grim but not unjust man now determined to acquire England and make his headquarters here, a richer land than his native Normandy. So he made his invasion.

He was opposed by King Harold, son of the formidable Earl Godwin who had for long been the leader of the English, and once again the Isle of Wight and the sea around it began to come into their own. Harold, like William himself, was essentially sea-minded, and he intended his ships to be the first line of defence. All through the summer of 1066, therefore, he kept his fleet plying between the Island and the Straits of Dover, not knowing how William intended to come, but rather expecting that he would try to secure that thoroughfare into the country which Asclepio-dotus and, allegedly, Cerdic long before had used. So, during the whole summer, his ships cruised about the Island and the Solent, and up-channel as far as the Straits. Thus, again and again, they must have cast anchor temporarily in the roadstead of Spithead.

William was ever noted for his cunning. He was not only a man of courage and determination but also of craft. He dared not risk crossing the Channel in the face of Harold's ships, but he sent a trader who spread the story that William had given up the invasion for that year owing to the late season. Harold, perhaps because he dearly wanted to do so, believed this false information, dispersed the fleet and set off at speed to deal with Tostig and Harald Hard-rada who had attacked Northumbria. After a resounding victory at Stamford Bridge, Harold learned that he had been deceived and that the Duke of Normandy, William the Bastard (as it was then his custom to sign himself) had made a safe landing in Sussex.

Harold wasted no time; he set out at once down the road from Stamford Bridge, forced-marching all the way and gathering in the fyrd or militia in the course of his long weary journey. William having made his unopposed landing at Pevensey between Beachy Head and Hastings, the contest after all resolved itself into a land encounter, with William's Norman knights opposed by Harold's unmounted hus-carles and his gallant English fyrd. As everyone knows, it was the cavalry and William's generalship which prevailed at the battle of Senlac or Hastings. The last champion of the old English fell, and William was King of England.

It was he who, in his last years, caused the Domesday survey to be made. This wonderful document makes it appear that even in 1086 Portsmouth did not yet exist as a town. We have seen that it already existed as a hamlet; had it been anything more, Domesday would surely not have failed to notice it, as it noticed the rival port of Southampton, now a town though still a small one. Of course, the land upon which Portsmouth stands is mentioned; for by then the whole of Saxon England was divided into manors, whose description was the object of the compilers of the Book. The acreage, for instance, of the manors of Buckland, Copnor and Fratton, all on Portsea Island, are there, each with one lord and a sprinkling of villeins, bordars and serfs; how many ploughs each lord possessed; how many cattle and swine each man owned; how much each had been worth in the time of Edward the Confessor and how much they were assessed at in 1086. All this; but no reference to Portsmouth as such.

Yet its blossoming could not now be far off. The very fact of the Norman Conquest meant that the importance of the whole area must now vastly increase. For the whole congeries of the Solent, Southampton Water, Portsmouth Harbour and so forth pointed straight at the Norman ports of Barfleur and Honfleur – to the other half of the possessions of William I. So instead of the Channel forming, as hitherto it had always done, a national frontier, it now became the highway between the two integral parts of the same kingdom. Whenever a Norman king of England wished to proceed to the other part of his dominions, he had to come down to Portsmouth Harbour or Southampton Water in order to get there.

Between the Conquest and the giving of the Charter to Portsmouth in 1194, this is exactly what the various kings were doing. Before the Conquest, such ships as the English possessed were based upon the ports in the Narrow Seas, the famous Cinque Ports – Sandwich, Dover, Hythe, Romney and Hastings, with Winchelsea and Rye added a little later. But after 1066, Southampton, Portchester and, later, Portsmouth were beginning to take their place, not only because they were strategically better placed but also because they offered much more suitable anchorages in much more sheltered waters. In fact, the naval centre of gravity of England was switching from Kent to Hampshire.

Moreover, once Portsmouth was in existence, it was a better naval port than Southampton, especially in the days of sail, when contrary winds often made departure difficult. And, by the same token, Spithead was a better anchorage – longer, wider and deeper – than Southampton Water. Both were sheltered enough, but it was a far shorter distance from Spithead to the open sea if – as often happened upon naval occasions – haste was of the essence. So when Portsmouth became the principal naval base, Spithead almost automatically became the principal naval anchorage. It is true that, only ten years after the giving of her charter to Portsmouth, the Angevin kings of England – notably the wilful and difficult King John – lost their original home of Normandy. But the English still retained much of what is now France, mainly to the south of Normandy, which itself passed under the sway of the King of a rising France who was becoming, and for long remained, England's most dangerous enemy. Thus the seat of England's naval power remained in Hampshire, and returned no more to the harbours of Kent.

*Chapter II*

# THE MIDDLE AGES

Even before Portsmouth obtained its Charter it was clear how things were going. In 1101 Duke Robert of Normandy, the Conqueror's eldest son, but something of a ne'er-do-well, having taken part in the First Crusade, returned home to learn that a younger son of his father had usurped his place on the throne of England. He gathered supporters to his flag, sailed into the Solent, crossed Spithead and landed at the still insignificant town of Portsmouth. His successful brother, Henry I, hurried down from London, and the rivals met at West Meon. Here Henry had the tact – and the power – to persuade Robert to renounce his title to the Crown, which Henry kept. Thereafter he was often at Portsmouth Harbour. In 1123, for instance, he was there – indeed probably at Spithead – on board a ship in which he was to cross to Normandy, and, from that front seat (where a contrary wind kept him for four whole weeks) he could hardly help admiring the great quiet stretch of water which gave so perfect a welcome to invaders. It was some years later that he took in hand the ruins of the old Roman fort at Portchester, repaired them, and added a keep. He (being a pious soul) also founded a priory of Augustinian canons within its walls. The castle remained, and remains to this day. The canons, however, soon found the site too noisy for them, and they moved across the Portsdown Hills to Southwick, where they built a new shrine, much visited by pilgrims until 1538, when Henry VIII, who disapproved of all such superstititions, incontinently closed it down.

But castle and priory are both signs of an increasing population. and Portsmouth was certainly growing when King Stephen came to the throne. Indeed, in 1139 formidable opposition landed there in the person of Henry I's daughter, the Empress Matilda, and her son, afterwards to be Henry II. But Stephen was much less successful in dealing with these interlopers than Henry I had been with his, and a disastrous civil war broke out which lasted for many years and ended only when young Henry had been nominated as Stephen's successor.

It was Henry II more than any other monarch who was responsible for the settlement's growth. His overseas dominions were at least as important to him as his English crown, and he was constantly passing from one to the other. Thus at least ten visits of his to Portsmouth are recorded, either going or coming: and it was finally from here that he departed for the last time. It is also alleged, though on rather doubtful authority, that he made his last will and testament on the very shores of Spithead.

It was Henry II's son, Richard the Lionheart (as mentioned earlier), who gave Portsmouth its earliest known Charter in 1194, five years after the old king's death. Thus Portsmouth was at last definitely in full existence, and it has since always remained so. But for quite a long time it had only a meagre existence, because it still had no port facilities to speak of. For a while, indeed, there were not even any docking facilities in anything like a modern sense. To the medieval mariner, in the words of the old definition,

a dock is any creek or place where we may cast in a ship out of the tideway into the ooze, and then, when the ship hath made herself a place to lie in, we say the ship hath docked herself.

Yet from Richard's time onwards the harbour began to become one of the principal assembly-points for English fleets. Richard built himself a house there, and there he collected the fleet in which he embarked for his great Crusade, though in the end it actually sailed from Dartmouth. And to Portsmouth he returned when released from his famous captivity at the hands of the Austrian Archduke and the Emperor Henry VI. This was in fact the moment when he granted the town his Charter. Immediately afterwards, he was off again, this time to punish the French King for his treachery during

Richard's imprisonment. Thereafter, with increasing frequency, Spithead became the rendezvous for overseas expeditions.

It would be interesting to know exactly where these expeditions lay when assembling. Some of them, we know, consisted of a very large number of ships, though of course most of the ships were small. Did they lie, we must wonder, inside the narrow entrance of the harbour? Or did they spill over into the far roomier anchorage of Spithead? It almost looks as though they did the latter. The Chroniclers, who constitute our only source of information, no doubt wildly exaggerated their numbers – figures of over a thousand, for instance, are not at all uncommon – but even allowing for the exuberance natural to such authorities, the fact seems certain that the numbers were sometimes very large indeed – in three figures, anyway. And the Portsmouth Harbour of those days did not offer very much room for ships, even for small ships, to lie up in – ships, that is, which did not want to 'dock in the ooze'. It consisted entirely of mudflats, uncovered at low water but submerged at the flood, with a few deeper natural channels which brought down the fresh water from the hinterland. And, though probably it would not greatly matter if at low water the ships grounded on the flats, there would still be very little room for hundreds of them. So what probably happened in the normal way was that, if the weather outside looked fair and there was no considerable sea coming in from the south-east (the only dangerous direction), they lay outside, but still close enough to the entrance to be able to scuttle into port if they smelt danger, either from the swell or from an approaching enemy. Indeed the great majority of these little ships, since they drew less than two fathoms of water, could safely anchor actually on the Spit Sand, which had that average depth, so that they had only a very short distance to run before they would be safely inside.

That this was the ordinary procedure seems to be confirmed by an episode which took place in 1242. By then, of course, the Lionheart was gone and so was his brother John Lackland. Now *his* son, Henry III, was king. In that year while he was campaigning in France he sent for a reinforcement which, like so many others, was to assemble at Spithead. The French king, knowing this, ordered his ships into the anchorage to prevent the reinforcement

42

from sailing. In due course they arrived off the harbour mouth unopposed, and proceeded, we are told, to blockade it. This is the first recorded occasion (apart from piratical raids) of warlike operations taking place in Spithead itself. The English ships, we must suppose, had seen the enemy fleet approaching, and scurried back into the harbour: for certainly none were caught outside. But details are lacking. All we know is that they succeeded in getting in. Moreover, having done so, they contrived somehow to get out again without the blockaders seeing them, and sailed clean away. The thwarted enemy followed them. But the wind rose to gale force, and both of the somewhat fragile fleets were sadly buffeted. The English ships, however, suffered rather more than the enemy, and crawled back to Portsmouth again. So, though the French fleet was damaged, Henry did not get his reinforcement after all, and his whole campaign was ruined.

To return to King John. A great huntsman, he devoted much time to the sport in the forests of Hampshire, and stayed at Portchester Castle no less than eighteen times. He was also very navy-conscious, giving his ships their first elementary organization. He instituted the office of 'Keeper of the King's Ships' (or, as sometimes called, 'Keeper of the Sea Ports') and appointed to the post William de Wrotham, who was also – in our eyes an odd mixture – Archdeacon of Taunton. This official resided for the most part at Portsmouth, and he is the first purely naval administrator whose name has survived. His duties included not only the fitting out and maintenance of the royal ships (though none were built at Portsmouth yet), but also a general supervision of the growing commercial traffic of the port.

In 1212 the primitive docks were slightly improved. John wrote to the Sheriff of Southampton:

We order you without delay to cause our docks at Portsmouth to be enclosed with a good and strong wall in a manner that our beloved and faithful William Archdeacon of Taunton will tell you. This is for the preservation of our ships and galleys. You are also to cause penthouses to be made to these walls in which all our ships tackle may be safely kept. Be as quick as you can, so

43

that the work may be completed this summer, and in the coming winter our ships and galleys and their rigging may not receive any damage.

In other words John ordered the Sheriff to build a security wall round the docks which already existed. Some have taken these orders to mean that the proposal was to build a quay or jetty, but it seems more likely that the purpose of the wall, apart from supporting the sheds, was to protect the stores against predatory local inhabitants. The only question is, who built the docks? King John? Or his brother Richard, as part of his scheme for the development of Portsmouth? In 1228 the docks collapsed, but the dockyard continued to be used for stores.

John had succeeded in 1204 in losing Normandy, largely by his own folly, so that the Solent ceased to be the direct route from one part of his dominions to the other. His frenzied attempts to recover his lost territory mostly started from Portsmouth, but, threatened now by the growing might of France over the narrow seas, he tended to have dealings once more with Sandwich, Dover and other old Channel ports.

Long after the Saxons and Danes had given up their marauding, piracy remained one of the greatest dangers not only to Portsmouth but to all the surrounding waters. There came a time when these pirates ceased to be merely lawless individuals, English as well as French and Flemish, and began to act in concert. Some – in fact the most pernicious of them all – were the seamen of the Cinque Ports who, from the late 1200s and right through the 1300s, made life intolerable for the men of both Portsmouth and Southampton. It was already a case of setting a thief to catch a thief. As time went on, although the Cinque Ports still provided the Crown with a set quota of fighting ships a year, those of their vessels which were not so employed spent more and more of their time hovering about the Solent and Spithead, attacking all shipping from the Isle of Wight and the adjacent mainland, and ruthlessly making the crews – their own countrymen – walk the plank.

The first climax of this rank piracy came after the defeat by Prince (afterwards King) Edward of Simon de Montfort and his barons when, deprived of some of their own Channel ports, a strong force of them sailed round to Portsmouth, fought its inhabitants in Spithead, defeated them, and, entering the town, captured and destroyed most of it. This was a sad set-back to the budding port, which did not fully recover for many years. It was mainly for this reason that the great King Edward I, when he ascended the throne, saw that he must tighten his hold not only over the approaches to Portsmouth but also over the whole of the Isle of Wight. For this purpose he appointed in 1294 to the Hampshire waters a strong-armed man, Sir William de Leybourne, who was the first Englishman to bear the title of Admiral, though not on that occasion nor on that account.[1] This formidable personage spent most of his time either at Spithead or in strictly Isle of Wight waters.

Leybourne did not, of course, extirpate piracy, even the local brand. The pirate is the legacy of all semi-civilized ages, and he always rears his ugly head whenever a Government is too weak to keep him under. But long before Leybourne could do much about it, the danger from pirates, as the prime enemy, had been replaced by the danger from France. The so-called Hundred Years' War in fact lasted for rather more than a century: and as France became our chronic enemy, she fixed longing eyes more and more upon the Isle of Wight. After all, Spithead is as vulnerable – as much threatened – from there as it is from the mainland of Hampshire. And it was largely, of course, due to Portsmouth's growing importance that France began to want to possess the Island.

She tried – for the first time seriously – to obtain it in 1337, when a mixed French and Scottish fleet attacked the English as they lay at anchor off the east end of the Island. Much damage was done on both sides, but the attempt was indecisive. The following year, however, there came a more determined and much more successful French attempt. Our enemies, under that great captain Nicholas Béhuchet, sailed boldly into Spithead, crossed it without opposition, and landed right in the town. One chronicler records that they

[1] His title while cruising round the Island was 'Captain of the King's Mariners'. He earned the title of 'Admiral of the Sea' afterwards when sent abroad by Edward on a diplomatic mission.

were dressed as Englishmen and carried English banners. But whether this be true or not, they were disastrously successful. They burnt the whole town except for the two principal churches, which survived probably because (unlike the rest of the buildings) they were built of stone. Then the inhabitants rallied, we are told, and drove the enemy back into Spithead – with enormous losses, says the chronicler. Yet they can hardly have been all that enormous, because Béhuchet went straight on and treated Southampton in exactly the same way.

Again, two years later, in 1340, the French landed in force on the island at St Helens, in an all-out attempt to take – and to keep – the Wight. But this time they failed because the King's Warden, Sir Theobald Russell, resisted so fiercely that, this time, they undoubtedly *were* driven into the sea, though the Warden himself was mortally wounded in the encounter. The result of these assaults was that both Southampton and Portsmouth built walls all round their towns. The relative importance of the two, however, may be measured by the fact that, whereas Southampton's fortifications were built of good solid masonry, much of which stands to this day, at Portsmouth the wall was composed of timber, brought from the Forest of Bere (which then came down almost to Portchester), held together with mud from the harbour. Of that earliest wall, it is hardly necessary to say, practically every trace has long since vanished. Portsmouth, however, was still not rich enough to provide a more permanent defence, and in 1369 the French landed again from Spithead and took and burned much of what the wretched citizens had erected since the last attack.

In the 1370s and early 1380s, the situation remained grim. The Admiral of France, Jean de Vienne, was virtually in control of the Channel, and twice more, in 1377 and 1380, he assaulted the all but defenceless town. He attacked Southampton too, but her stone walls saved her. The attack of 1377, delivered mainly upon the Isle of Wight, was a very touch-and-go affair. The enemy landed on the north shore of the Island, burnt Yarmouth and Newtown, and then proceeded to lay siege to the Castle of Carisbrooke. It was most gallantly defended by the Constable, Sir Hugh Tyrell, and at length the French retreated from the only set siege the Castle has ever sustained.

Only once – in 1386 – did the men of Portsmouth turn on the enemy, and carry the war into their territory. On that occasion they allied themselves with the people of Dartmouth and penetrated up the Seine with a combined force, doing considerable damage there. At the very end of the century things improved a little. Richard II and after him Henry IV erected fortifications (though probably still only wooden ones) at the entrance to the harbour. And they were much more effective when the French, now led by the Comte de St Pol, had another go at the Island in 1403. Taking it by surprise, he occupied most of it, and demanded a huge ransom. While waiting for this, St Pol crossed Spithead and suddenly attacked Portsmouth; but, it seems, he was daunted by the sight of the new tower at the harbour mouth, and retreated. Thereupon the men of Portsmouth, joining with those of Southampton, sallied forth from their defences and landed on the Island, taking St Pol by surprise and compelling him to leave in a hurry and without his ransom.

Henry V, the victor of Agincourt, was probably more sea-minded than any of his predecessors, and it was he who introduced ship-building into south Hampshire. But not to Portsmouth, which was now lagging far behind its rival, the well-defended, stone-walled Southampton. It was therefore this town that he preferred as a base for his French wars. He soon became aware, too, of the advantages for shipbuilding in the Hamble River, which flows into Southampton Water. In his day, this stream, with its fine anchorage at Bursledon, became the site of a real, though short-lived, shipbuilding industry. Here he built some of the finest and biggest vessels that England had ever possessed. The best fitted-out, though perhaps not the largest, was called the *Grace Dieu*, a ship whose burden was at least 400 tons.[1] The sad remains of this great and experimental ship, destroyed by fire in 1439, still lie in the estuary

[1] It may well have been even greater than this. It is almost impossible to estimate the true carrying capacity of medieval English ships. Thus its tonnage is mentioned only twice in official papers: once it is 400 tons; once 1400. See M. Oppenheim, *Administration of the Royal Navy*, p. 12 n.

47

of the Hamble River. Still, Portsmouth, though its nose was temporarily put out of joint by its rival, yet shared some of its glory; and it was from Portchester that, after considerable delay, the King at length sailed for the campaign of Agincourt – with, it would seem, not less than 1,400 vessels of all sorts. Throughout that famous campaign Spithead was much in the picture, for all these 1,400 ships must have passed across its waters at one time or another. Indeed, it is very doubtful whether the larger vessels ever entered Portsmouth Harbour at all. It is much more likely that they waited for the King outside, riding at anchor on the broad bosom of Spithead.

In naval matters Henry V was a long way ahead of his time, but when he died at a very early age (only seven years after Agincourt), his successor made no attempt to maintain his great ships, which were immediately sold for a mere song to pay off the dead king's debts. For more than half a century, indeed, naval policy was sadly neglected.

When Henry V's successor came to the throne he was less than a year old, and, in the inevitably chaotic period that followed, both the Solent ports lapsed into wholesale piracy again, and even at times into wholesale murder. At Portsmouth in 1450, for instance, a very nasty affair occurred. In that year war with France broke out again, and the King sent down his minister, Adam de Moleyns, Bishop of Chichester, to pacify certain mutinous seamen who were complaining of many years' arrears of pay. He had no more than arrived, however, when an infuriated mob of sailors set upon the unfortunate man and stoned him to death in broad daylight outside the church-hospital of Domus Dei. It was a tragic and indeed futile business, all the more ironical because the Bishop was particularly fond of the sea, ships and sailors; an advocate, moreover, of a judicious use of the sea (he was probably the author of *The Libel of English Policie*, the earliest known book to point out the value to England of sea-power). The medieval church reacted swiftly and savagely to the outrage. The whole town was excommunicated, and remained so for nearly sixty years. The ban was finally removed only in 1508.

But now Portsmouth's worst days were over, and all improvement must be attributed to the first Tudor King. Soon after Henry

4. Portsmouth from Gosport, 1749, looking across the Harbour at the Dockyard and town. Through the Harbour entrance can be seen the fleet in Spithead, with the hills of Wight on the right above Fort Blockhouse

5. Portsmouth Point, 1801

6. Boat-repairing on the shore at Portsmouth

VII seized the throne on Bosworth Field, the French nation at last achieved unity by the incorporation of Brittany with its Crown in 1491. France now held the whole of the Channel coast facing England, and the whole of the Atlantic coast down almost to the Pyrenees. Henry, himself a usurper, was forced to look seriously to his naval defences. Southampton by this time had already developed into a real commercial port. What Henry had to find was a strictly naval one. Inevitably he chose Portsmouth, because French power now spread far beyond the Straits of Dover, and the Solent was once more the area which faced squarely upon the growing might of France.

He first built up the defences of the place in stone, erecting the Round Towers at the harbour entrance. But his greatest innovation was to start building, in 1495, the first dock which by any stretch of the imagination could be called a modern one. For good measure, it was a dry dock to facilitate underwater repairs, and it was the first of its kind in England and probably in the world. It had timber sides – 4,524 feet of planking were used in its construction[1] – and an inner and an outer gate. Once a ship had entered, the gates were closed, the space between them sealed with stones and clay, and the water pumped out of the dock. The cost was £193 0s 6¾d. It was perhaps clumsy, but it served its purpose. The first ship put into it was the very large (for that day) *Sovereign*, and the next was the even larger *Regent*. Once more it is hardly possible to assess the tonnage of this famous ship, but it is quite clear that she was at least as large as any previous King's Ship.[2] She also drew more water; so much so that they may have had to dredge a passage for her up to the new dry dock. Since she could no longer come in at will over the Spit Sand, she must have entered by the deep channel which ran (and runs) to the east of it. Out at the ordinary anchorage at Spithead, however, questions of draught did

---

[1] M. Oppenheim (ed.), *Accounts and Inventories of Henry VII* (Navy Records Society, 1896, vol. viii), pp. xxxvi-xxxix.

[2] Orders survive for her construction, in which her projected tonnage is given as 600. But she may well have been more than this. Sir Edward Howard said in 1512 that she displaced one thousand tons. See *The French War of 1512–13* (Navy Records Society, 1897, vol. x), p. xiv.

not arise at all, for there, centuries later, super-dreadnoughts could lie quite comfortably.

In Henry VII's time, too, the first King's Ship ever to be constructed at Portsmouth was built in the new dock. She was named the *Sweepstake*, and is down as costing £231.[1] Compared with the *Regent* and the *Sovereign*, she was a very small craft indeed.

This King owned, first and last, only thirteen ships: he inherited six with the crown, acquired two more by purchase, and thus new-built only five. But he used the fleet in a novel way. From time to time he hired merchantmen from his richer subjects, and let them out along with his own royal ships to other subjects. Being a shrewd businessman, he made so much profit from these transactions that it is said (albeit on rather uncertain authority) he 'died worth two million golden sovereigns'. This he may well have done, if only because he was a most astute financier operating in a community of much less astute ones: and also, it may as well be owned, because he actually invented the sovereign.

His son, the much-discussed Henry VIII, partly because he inherited this sum – huge for those days – but also because in his time he made even more money by such debatable operations as dissolving the monasteries, was able to own no less than ninety-nine ships, mostly built by himself. So he may well be called, as he so often is, the true founder of the Royal Navy. They were mostly sailing ships of various sizes: that is, eighty-six of them were. The other thirteen were what he called 'roo barges' – row-barges, or vessels propelled by oars, and similar in general design to (though at about 20 tons much smaller than) the galleys which constituted the spearhead of the fleets of his foreign rivals. These will be described later and in greater detail. But let us look first at the sailing ships. They were built on lines not dissimilar to those of the *Regent*, and they varied in size from the little *Hare* of some 30 tons to the pride of his fleet, the immense *Henry Grâce à Dieu*, popularly called 'The Great Harry', of probably at least 1,000 tons. And not only did he vastly enlarge his fleet, but in 1527 he enlarged Portsmouth dockyard to cope with it.

[1] *Accounts and Inventories of Henry VII* (Navy Records Society, 1896, vol. viii), p. 35.

It has been necessary to say a word about his fleet in order to explain the course of the one and only pitched battle fought wholly in Spithead. For that purpose too, one must know something of the political lay-out of Western Europe in Henry VIII's day. During most of his reign that busy king was engaged in wars with his ambitious rival, Francis I of France, or, when he was not fighting him, in striving to keep the balance between the two most important continental families of Valois (France) and Habsburg (Austria, and later Spain). These two, in the persons of Francis of France and the Habsburg Emperor, Charles V, were already bidding fair to dominate all Europe.

Henry began with a brisk war against France, during which, in 1512, he lost, among other things, his father's 'Great Ship' the *Regent*, which was burnt in action with the French *Cordelière* off Brest. Both ships, grappled in a deadly embrace, went up in flames which no man could control.[1] Her commanding officer, Sir Thomas Knyvet, perished in the fire, but 180 of her people were rescued, while there were only six survivors from the *Cordelière*.

Much is made in the chronicles of that day of the famous and extravagant meeting near Calais in 1520 which is known as 'The Field of the Cloth of Gold'. But this, in spite of all the immense display lavished upon it, was so much eye-wash and ended very soon in stalemate. Far more important was the visit the Emperor Charles V made to Henry very shortly afterwards, when the citizens of Portsmouth, lining the shores of Spithead, beheld a vast fleet of 180 ships sailing across it *en route* for Southampton, where Charles was – much less expensively – entertained for nearly a week. Whereas no result emerged from the much-vaunted Field, Charles's visit to Southampton led to an alliance which lasted more or less unbroken for the better part of sixty years. Henry had thrown in his lot with Spain and Austria, and for the rest of his life he fought against France.

It was during his third war with her in 1544 that he erected, on the shore of Spithead itself, that strong defensive work known as

[1] See *The French War of 1512–13* (Navy Records Society, vol. x), pp. xxv-xxvi.

Southsea Castle.[1] In that year, too, he succeeded in capturing the town of Boulogne, which was such a blow to Francis that he decided, the following year, to retaliate with an all-out assault on Portsmouth and the Isle of Wight.

[1] The Castle is still there. In fact, in 1967 it was restored and turned into a museum.

# Chapter III

# ACTIONS FOUGHT IN OR NEAR SPITHEAD

A. *The Battle of Spithead, 1545*

With the full intention, then, of capturing and holding the Isle of Wight, Francis sent out his Admiral, D'Annibault, with a huge armada of 150 great sailing-transports carrying, it is said, 60,000 men. But this fleet of sailing-ships was not his true fighting navy. That was a force of seventy-five oared craft, including a squadron of those wicked-looking vessels known in the Mediterranean as galleys.

This type of vessel, though it carried one mast, a long yard and a large fore-and-aft triangular sail (for use when not in action) was essentially a ship propelled by oars, manned by galley-slaves chained to their benches. The length of the boat was something like eight times its breadth: it had one deck only, and it lay low in the water, with a very low freeboard – these features being essential concomitants to all oared vessels. Over the whole length of its stout keel there ran a gangway, where the slave-overseers stalked up and down wielding long whips, to 'encourage' the slaves. The forward extremity of the keel projected beyond the bows, and just above the waterline. It was pointed, and shod with iron. This was the galley's principal offensive weapon, the whole ship being manoeuvred by its galley-master so as to ram the enemy's vessel, if possible amidships, cutting clean through it. Owing to the ship's low freeboard, there was no room for any guns on the broadside, the whole length of which was taken up by its motive power – the oars. But it did have, lying across the bows, a platform on which was mounted a battery of (usually) five guns, all facing forward.

The four outer ones, however, were light-weight pieces, designed to kill or wound men rather than sink ships. But the middle gun, which recoiled straight backwards down the length of its very solid keel, was a large and powerful weapon: a potential ship-killer. There was also, aft, another platform, placed across the stern. This was for the officers' use, and for the numerous soldiers who were always on board. As, however, no guns were ever mounted on it, it followed that all the galley's offensive weapons faced straight forward; and that that was the only direction in which it could strike. On board a typical galley of the period manned for war, there were usually, apart from the officers, something like 230 soldiers and 140 galley-slaves. It carried virtually no mariners at all.

This was the age-old weapon of war used in the navies of all Mediterranean countries. They had used this kind of ship to fight all their battles at sea for something like the last two thousand years: for the ships of Athens and Sparta, as well as those of Rome, were approximately of this sort. It follows from this that a complete, and even complicated, set of naval tactics existed, as well as quite a considerable corpus of works on the subject. In other words, those states which used galleys to fight with – and that was most states in Europe *except* England – knew, or thought they knew, exactly how to use them. They all, of course, possessed other ships – ships which used the winds of heaven as their motive power – but they used such sailing-ships only for the purpose of trade: never for war. For war they used only their galleys.

The sailing merchantmen were naturally of a very different type. They were heavily built with massive timbers, riding very high in the water and infinitely more 'tubby' than galleys. They were so short in their build – being barely twice, or at most two and a half times, as long as they were broad – that, what with the lee-wardliness of their high sides, they were quite wretched sailers; while the yards which carried the sails could be turned only slightly, so that they could hardly sail against, or even across, the wind at all. They were, therefore, too hopelessly unmanoeuvrable to be of any use in a battle. So their owners simply did not use them for such a purpose, relying, when action was required, entirely upon their galleys. This, then, was the well-nigh universal rule – for fighting, rowed galleys; for carrying goods for trade, these tub-like ships which, unlike the galleys, had roomy holds for the carriage of goods. And such was the practice in almost every foreign country.

From the first, however, England had pursued a very different policy. From time immemorial we had used sailing ships – originally very like the foreign merchantmen – to the exclusion of all other types. It is, of course, no accident that the Latin words for a warship were *Navis Longa* – the long ship; that is, the Galley. But when Englishmen used those words (which was not often) they were referring, as likely as not, to the mainly oar-propelled 'drakars' which had once brought the Danes over to this country. We ordinarily called our craft 'Tall Ships', referring presumably to the height of their masts. But we might have called them (as later writers have done) 'Round Ships', for, though never, of course, literally circular, they were, contrasted with the galley's eight-to-one ratio, comparatively circular. The dimensions of the old English sailing-ship, or 'Cog', might well be only two breadths to one length. This ship, like the foreign merchant ship, was a most 'tubby' vessel, built of very thick plank, standing very high out of the water, and furnished – originally – with a single mast and a single sail. And originally – like the foreign sailing-ship – it was an exceedingly poor sailer, exceedingly leewardly, and a really hopeless proposition to manoeuvre in: therefore a hopeless man-of-war.

But it was the cog that we had always persevered with, and when we wanted to use it for fighting in, we had experimented with it; pulling it out, as it were, to something like three or three-and-a-half breadths to its length, in order to make it a better sailer. Gradually, too, we had improved its sailing power by adding fresh masts and sails, and we had contrived, by adding movable yards, to coax it into sailing a good deal closer to the wind than it had done originally. It could now sail, in fact, comparatively 'close-hauled'. So we had little or no truck with the galley, which, no doubt, we found unusable for too many days in the year because of our boisterous weather and its unseaworthiness – it could not readily stand up to the long waves and the heavy swells of our home waters. To sum up, Henry VII's *Regent*, and still more Henry VIII's *Great Harry*, were both developments of the medieval cog, and had very little in common with the classical galley.

Each type, though, had its own strengths and its own weaknesses. The galley had one potentially great advantage – it possessed free movement: it could proceed in any direction it wished at any time it liked. It could even be rowed dead into the eye of the wind. So, when well and skilfully handled, it was a highly manoeuvrable craft, and therefore (theoretically) a relatively fine tactical weapon. On the other hand, the typical English ship (which has gradually acquired the generic name of 'galleon') had *no* free movement. Indeed, even when, in the early nineteenth century, it reached its fullest development, it could never sail, even when as close-hauled as possible, within six points on either side of the wind. It was always, then – as compared with the galley – a poor tactical performer.

Yet it did have over-riding advantages over the galley when it came to strategy. As compared with its main rival, it was thoroughly sea-worthy; with its high freeboard it could ride out gales which would instantly prove fatal to the galley. It could in fact keep at sea long after the galley had to run for shelter, or face the risk of sinking. Then again, it had, relatively, a high degree of sea-endurance. Its capacious holds could stow away provisions for months on end, where the galley-user (who found he had very little storage-space) would have to return to port or starve.

But what really ensured in the end that the galleon should prevail over the galley was the triumph of the gun as a weapon of war. As the whole art of gunnery improved, it soon became clear that the sailing-ship could carry a far heavier battery of such weapons than the oared vessel ever could. Once the hull of the galleon had been pierced to allow for portholes (which happened around the year 1500) the number of pieces of artillery which could be mounted on its two broadsides was almost unlimited: on as many as three decks too. So it happened that the later ships of the galleon type could – – and did – carry well over 100 guns, of various calibres, whereas the unfortunate galley was confined to *one* heavy one – or at most two, if it mounted one facing aft over its keel.

It was then the advent of the gun which in the end decided the issue, establishing the galleon as the master of the galley. But it took a long time to happen, and, in 1545, the issue was by no means decided, mainly because, at that time, the potentialities of the galleon were more or less unknown. Even the English, to a great extent its inventors, were still quite ignorant of how best to use it. We have seen that galley tactics – two thousand years of them – were very highly developed, and admirably understood by galley-users. But sailing-ship tactics were still quite unknown, and so galleon-users still had to rely, painfully, on trial and error.

Herein lies the great nautical and naval interest in this clash of galley and galleon. The Battle of Spithead was in fact the very first occasion when the two diametrically opposed systems met in mortal conflict. The principal interest lies in this fact, and not in the result of the action. That, one is bound to admit, was in no way spectacular. In fact, it was distinctly dull. It is almost always so when new weapons of warfare first come into use: the first submarine to appear in action – when Nelson's Hardy in his flagship the *Ramillies* in the 1812–15 American War was attacked by one – spluttered out like a damp squib; the first use of an armoured gun-turret – in the duel in the American Civil War between the Confederate *Merrimac* and the Federal *Monitor* – ended quite comically with practically no damage done on either side; the first firing in anger of a Whitehead torpedo – launched by our flagship the *Shah* against the Peruvian rebel the *Huascar* – was similarly farcical because, although the *Shah* fired her 'fish' with unerring accuracy, travelling at 9 knots, the *Huascar*, by simply running away at 11 knots, easily won the race. Even on land it was the same: the British lost all the value of surprise when they unleashed too few of that potential war-winning invention, the tank, at the enemy on the Western Front in 1917, while the Germans did just the same when they attacked the Canadians in 1915 with the first gas assault. So was the first fight between galleon and galley in Spithead a sad fiasco.[1]

D'Annibault got across the English Channel unopposed. For, in boisterous weather, a portion of Henry's fleet under Lord Seymour

[1] A good account of the action is to be found in Sir Julian Corbett, *Drake and the Tudor Navy*, vol. I, pp. 46–50.

had vainly tried to destroy the French with fireships, but had given up the attempt and returned to base (which was Spithead). So long as the English fleet was all assembled together in the anchorage, D'Annibault did not think it safe to bring up his transports with the 60,000 infantry on board. Instead, he anchored in St Helens Roads with his galleys and such other fighting sailing-ships as he had with him (Plate 1), and sent on to Spithead an advance-guard of four galleys under the command of Paulin, Baron de la Garde, the most distinguished galley-leader of that day. They advanced rather cautiously across Spithead. The combined English fleet, about one hundred strong, and now under their proper leader, Lord Lisle, stood out on a land wind to meet them. Throughout all the actions which followed, Henry himself was present in Southsea Castle, where he had a ring-side view of the fighting. But he never went on board any of his ships, leaving the active command to Lisle.

The English at the start pressed on boldly. D'Annibault, seeing this, threw in his entire galley-force, which, of course, though to leeward of the English fleet as it came down-wind, had no difficulty at all in approaching it up-wind. A desultory action at long range took place, and lasted until nightfall. Each side seemed to be distinctly nervous of the other. Then, fearing that they would not be able to make their anchorage again against the wind, the English ships broke off the action, and retired as best they could, helped now by the usual sou-westerly which generally got up in the evening. So they reached their anchorage safely; which was, it would seem, not on the present mooring-place at all, but in the entrance-channel to the east of the Spit Sand, and so right under the guns of Southsea Castle and of other more temporary batteries planted on the shore to the east of the Castle. They had chosen quite a good position, because the enemy could not out-flank them – had they tried, they would have stuck on the shallows of the Horse and Dean. Yet, strong as the position was, Lisle seems to have been content to anchor his fleet of sailing-broadside ships in line abreast!

Now in itself, one would have thought, this was quite extra-ordinary. All those sailing ships had virtually all their guns on their broadsides, so that, had they used what was by far their most telling armament, the whole of the roundshot would have been fired at point blank range straight into their next-door neighbours: in effect, their broadsides could not be fired at all!

This must have been the result of sheer inexperience on Lisle's part. None the less one would have expected him to realize the futility of it. And why did he not? Because, of course, Line Abreast was the standard formation of a galley-fleet, whose weakness always lay in the absence of any broadside at all. It therefore always tried to protect its flanks which were so vulnerable because there lay its oars, its total motive power. The galley, we recall, simply had to attack along the line of its advance, but a sailing-fleet's line of attack was (it seems fairly obvious now) diametrically opposite to a galley-fleet's – it could only develop its main fire-power at right angles to its line of advance. All this shows very forcibly how rudimentary were contemporary sailing-ship tactics! No doubt Lisle had read many treatises on naval tactics, but they were clearly all treatises on galley-tactics. On the handling of a fleet of sailing-ships in action there was nothing of any sort to read.

D'Annibault pursued the English until he was quite close to the Southsea shore. And then – perhaps fortunately for us – he made precisely the same mistake as Lisle, and doubtless for the same reason. He drew up his sailing-ships (of which he had quite a number) facing ours in line abreast, and only just within range. His galleys he sent in as an advance guard, with orders to engage the English fleet as closely as possible. And this task they performed, we are told, 'brilliantly'. But not very effectively, because there was only one safe course open to them. If they had rowed their ships into the intervals of Lisle's line abreast, they would have exposed themselves to the close fire of England's only weapon, which otherwise could not be used at all. Likewise using their main weapons and ramming the English galleons would have been quite suicidal, for even the rams, stout and sharp as they were, could not hope to do any real execution upon the massy timbers and the sheer weight of large sailing-ships. So they could really do nothing but fire upon the enemy, each ship with its one great gun, fired forwards. This they did: and, seeing that the English ships

could not reply with any great-gun fire at all, they seem to have
annoyed them considerably – and annoyed Henry too as he watched
from Southsea Castle. They had also been told to retire slowly as
they fought, in order, if possible, to lure the English away from
under the land-based guns, and out into the open water. This too
they did, and the English were lured. But, unfortunately for the
galleys, the normal morning land-wind began at that moment to
blow, so that, quite suddenly, Lisle was able to order his ships to
slip cables: and the galleys were still so near the English fleet that
they found themselves in imminent danger of having the tables
turned upon them and of being rammed by the sailing-ships! So
they turned as best they could – which, by the way, was rather a
poor best, because their great length allowed them to turn but
slowly. Then they rowed away, hoping still that Lisle would follow
them. This turning of galleys was a difficult and unpopular move
among their Captains because, if actually caught during the rather
lengthy operation, their fate would have been certain – the sheer
weight of one of Henry's great galleons would have been much
more than they could have withstood. And, though admittedly the
Great Ship made a peculiarly unhandy rammer, a near miss on
either side would have been just as good, and almost equally fatal
to the galley: for though the bows of the sailing-ship might well
miss the slender galley itself, the chances were much more in favour
of them slicing off all her oars on one side or the other, and so
depriving her of her whole motive power and reducing her to utter
impotence. Still, on this occasion the galleys were brilliantly
handled, and not one of them was either rammed by the English or
touched in their oars.

At this juncture, however, the French 'oared pieces' received a
sudden and unpleasant shock which (one would have thought)
should have revealed another fatal weakness in the galleys. Lord
Lisle's great ships ceased to pursue, and, as they lost way, out from
between them shot Henry's whole squadron of 'roo-barges' –
which, as has been told, were tiny editions of galleys. Their big
French sisters were now in full retreat – in line-abreast, of course –
and so found themselves at the mercy even of such insignificant
wasps. For, having no weapons whatever mounted aft, they could

not retaliate in any way. It was a most humiliating position to be in. Impertinently the little 20-tonners gave chase, coming right up to the galleys and pouring what shot they had, with complete impunity, into their sterns, which were unarmed and totally unprotected. Somehow they had to attempt the slow process of getting their bows round to face the enemy, during which time they suffered a good chance of being rammed by the roo-barges. At last, however, the best-known of all galley-captains, the illustrious Strozzi himself, contrived to put on a great spurt and so to give himself the opportunity to turn. Once that was accomplished, the role of the English roo-barges was over. They instantly turned – with ease, because they were such short boats – and, long before Strozzi could come up with them, they had bolted for safety behind the English Great Ships.

And here, substantially, the action ended. D'Annibault, it is true, tried to bring out the English fleet by landing some of his troops on the Island. But Wight was strongly held, the attack was rather half-hearted, and Lisle (or more properly Henry) refused to engage his ships again in such enclosed waters, where conditions were so admirably suited to galley warfare. So, in the end, D'Annibault re-embarked his soldiers and sailed away.

Lisle did not follow him, perhaps because of an unfortunate accident which had befallen one of Henry's Great Ships. At some moment during the battle – but which moment exactly is not known – the *Mary Rose* came to an untimely end, and sank with nearly all her men. It was the only considerable loss which either fleet sustained, and more will be said about it in a later chapter – a chapter which deals, not, like this, with actions, but with accidents. For it is quite clear that the loss of the *Mary Rose* was in no way caused by the enemy. It is clear too, that at no time during the battle did the galleys use their main weapons – their rams – and it is equally clear that the Great Ships did not once use theirs – their broadsides. The galleys, however, did do some execution with their secondary weapons – their guns; and those mosquito-craft, the roo-barges, did discomfit the galleys, revealing their weakness. And that was all.

This was not the end of the fighting for that year: but since the subsequent fighting did not take place in Spithead, it does not really earn more than a passing mention here. Yet, in the story of *Oar* v. *Sail* its importance was much too great to be omitted altogether.

Henry VIII, undergoing in Southsea Castle the humiliation of having to watch his beloved Great Ships being pounded by the great guns of the French galleys, had instant doubts about the wisdom of pitting sailing-ships against oared vessels: and even before the fight was over he had issued orders for the hurried production of a squadron of 'oared pieces'. This, we now know, was certainly retrograde. But that is to be wise after the event – we know *now* that the future lay with sails and not with oars. But no one knew it then. When Henry ordered things, however, they tended to get done: and only two months later Lisle was out in the English Channel again with, in addition to his 'main battle' of heavy sailing-ships, a 'vantward' consisting of 'oared pieces'. The fleets were destined to meet again, but off Shoreham in Sussex and not the Wight. And this time it is the rather scratch lot of the new squadron that receives honourable mention. But it is significant that the ships picked out for special notice by Lord Lisle were very far from being galleys. They were quite the latest sailing-ships to be added to Henry's Navy. And in the action off Shoreham they certainly acted as sailing-ships. In his report to the King, Lisle wrote:

... the *Mistress* and the *Anne Gallant* did so handle the galleys, *as well with their sides as with their prows*, that your Great Ships in a manner had little to do.

This can only mean one thing – that, off Shoreham on August 15, 1545, the Royal Navy fired in anger its first broadside: that essentially English weapon which was destined to win Britain her Empire.

B. *The Armada: The Fight Off Spithead*

Sail and oar did not meet again in full-scale conflict for another forty-two years: and then the protagonists were no longer England and France, but England and Spain – the Spain of Philip II.

In 1587, Sir Francis Drake raided the Spanish coast with a mixed force of Queen's Ships and merchantmen, all sailing-craft. This was that celebrated affair known to history as 'Singeing King Philip's Beard'. He boldly entered Cadiz Harbour, where he encountered a squadron of the real Spanish Navy, then composed exclusively of galleys. The fight which followed was curiously decisive. The galleys attacked the Queen's galleons but made no impression upon them whatsoever. Moreover, although the action took place in a confined stretch of water where, according to all the continental pundits of that day, the galleys should have prevailed without any difficulty at all, they did not. Contrary to all Spanish expectations, the guns of Drake's broadsides made them look quite innocuous, and 'El Draque' put them to flight with almost ridiculous ease. The effect of this action upon naval warfare in general, and upon the Spanish fleet in particular was staggering and permanent. Philip, now committed up to the neck in his great Enterprise of England, perceived at once, and with serious alarm, that he could not possibly use his professional fleet – his oared galleys – against England at all. So he was compelled – unless he would give up his schemes then and there – to collect hurriedly a scratch force composed almost exclusively of sailing-ships.

One must say *almost* exclusively, though, because he could not bring himself all at once to scrap the whole of his beloved regular navy. Thus, when his Invincible Armada sailed in the following year, it was composed of some 130 of such sailing-ships as he could assemble from all his many dominions, doubtfully reinforced by *eight* vessels whose motive power was still, partly at least, the oar. Thus he sent out four galleys proper – but in practice this small contingent failed to reach the English Channel, and gratefully sought shelter in neutral French ports. The other four, which soldiered on – and indeed which played no small part in the venture – belonged to a new type of ship altogether known as the 'galleasse', which was the Spanish idea of a compromise between oar and sail. They were, in their way, very formidable craft. They were rather more like galleys than galleons. They had the long, strong keel of the former, prolonged into a ram; and they had on each side, near the waterline, the slave-rowers' benches with a tier

63

of long, heavy projecting sweeps. But they had certain galleon features too. The rowing-deck was covered in, with another deck on top of it and masts, yards and sails above that. There was also a broadside of very heavy guns, all mounted on this upper deck above the oars. They were more seaworthy than the galleys, yet less so than the galleons, mainly because they carried so much of their weight too high. They did, however, have almost all of the galley's free movement – they could be propelled quite independently of the wind. And this ability made them very formidable opponents once or twice in the course of the long-drawn-out battles. The whole fleet was supplied with heavy artillery – heavier than the English possessed. But not one of the Spanish ships either sailed or manoeuvred nearly so well as their opponents. All but the galleasses (hardly suited to Channel weather because of their low freeboards) stood high out of the water with heavily-built superstructures, and they were very inferior sailers to the true 'galleon-type' of the English fleet.

The Duke of Medina Sidonia, the Spanish Commander-in-Chief, had very little knowledge of the sea, or experience in command upon it, and had at first been very unwilling to take on the responsibility because (he alleged) he was always sea-sick. But he was a high-born Grandee of Spain, who in honour virtually had to accept the post: moreover one who, owing to his inexperience, was perhaps the more to his master's liking. He clung to his orders with a pertinacity which (though rather wooden) was much to his credit. Those orders, drummed into his mind by Philip, were peremptory – to keep his unwieldy fleet together in as tight a formation as possible. His best ships – the Portuguese Royal fleet and the galleons of the Indian Guard of Castile, formed his 'main battle', and they led the fleet in line abreast, with only three galleasses ahead of them. Four squadrons of his next-best ships, sailing *en échelon* yet still each in squadron line abreast, brought up the rear, the Vanguard on the starboard wing, the Rearguard on the port wing. Between them were massed his 'hulks' – transports and storeships – carrying the bulk of his large army, which consisted of all Spain's best soldiers to the number of 19,000. In that order they reached the mouth of the Channel, and in that order the Duke

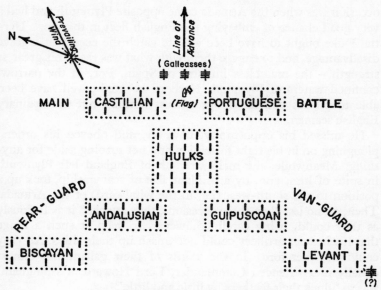

3. The formation of the Armada

commanded them to proceed right up it until they came to the
Narrows, where, on the flat coasts of Flanders, his co-adjutor, the
Duke of Parma, waited to join hands with him. Those were his
orders, very strict ones too, and it is only fair to the memory of the
Spanish Commander-in-Chief to place it on record that, in spite
of his almost total lack of experience, and a considerable battering
from the English fleet, he succeeded very largely in carrying them
out. So in that order the Armada at last reached the Straits of
Dover. True, those orders were foolish enough: Philip should
have known that the man on the spot *must* be given some latitude to
fight his own action, instead of being bound to obey a set of rules
made for him in Madrid, which took no cognizance about what the
enemy might or might not do. But that is how it was, so perhaps
the principal blame for what followed should be laid at the King's
door.

Twice at least during that long journey up-Channel, Medina
Sidonia should certainly have made other dispositions. The first

occasion was when the Armada came opposite Plymouth and had a very good chance of embaying the English fleet in that port. Here the Duke ought to have been able to catch the enemy at a grave disadvantage, and to engage them with what was really his greatest strength – the matchless infantry of Spain. For, in the narrow, confined waters of Plymouth Harbour he might well have been able to pit his veteran troops against nothing but the ordinary English seaman.

He missed his opportunity, however, and obeyed his orders, ploughing on in his tight formation and not turning aside for anything. Meanwhile, the main strength of England left Plymouth in spite of him, and, by a brilliant feat of seamanship, took up a position to the south-west (i.e. to the windward) of the Armada. Then, on no less than three occasions, they attacked it as furiously as they could, being careful, however, to keep at such a range that his heavier artillery could not smash up their ships. All they could do, therefore, (in the words of their gallant but almost equally inexperienced Commander, Lord Howard of Effingham) was to 'pluck their feathers by little and little'.

The first action took place off Plymouth itself: the second off Portland Bill. The third was off the Isle of Wight, which is, of course, the one which we must concentrate upon here. In neither of the first two did the English make any lasting impression upon that very orderly Spanish array. Nor in fact did they on the third occasion. But now strategical considerations began to count for more even than tactical ones.

Sidonia's advisers – all the best seamen in Spain – had, all the way up the Channel, been trying to persuade him that, before it was too late, he *must* break away from the King's orders. For they saw clearly enough that it was no good for the Armada to reach the Narrows before it was quite sure that Parma was ready in an instant to join it. After all, the whole purpose of the expedition was for the Armada to give cover to that prince's army, and to see it safely across the Channel to the coast of Kent. The trouble as they saw it – and at last he did too – was that, once they had proceeded eastwards beyond the Isle of Wight, there was no place at all where they could rest and shelter if Parma were so much as a day late in his preparations. The coast of Flanders was quite bare and harbourless for so many and such great ships as composed the Armada, and the shoals all along the shore made dangerous lying-ground everywhere. But rest and shelter was there for the asking at the quiet anchorage of Spithead. It was indeed an ideal place at which to stop and wait. 'Go there, therefore', said all his advisers. 'Cover yourself by landing troops on the Island, and you can sit there in perfect security, and wait for Parma (within limits) for as long as you like'. And even Sidonia saw the wisdom in what they said; so much so that he at last made up his mind to disobey the procrustean rules which had hitherto bound him. He would enter Spithead, lie there for a while, and in the meantime land on the Island. After all, it was still in living memory that this was what the French had done – or tried to do – in old King Harry's day.

So – in 1588 – both sides had a very clear local objective – the Duke to enter Spithead; the English, if they could, to push him past it. It is this fact which provides the great interest and importance to the fighting on Thursday, July 28, 1588.

When dawn broke on that day the Invincible Armada, still in almost perfect formation, was sailing along the southern shore of the Island, as close to the land as they dared, proposing, as soon as they reached its eastern end, to swing away to the north, cross St Helens Road, and occupy the anchorage of Spithead. The English were certainly aware of their intention, and they might without difficulty (such was their sailing superiority) have crept past the enemy and reached the entrance to the Solent before them. But, hitherto, the whole of their tactics had consisted in keeping to the windward – i.e. to the west – of the Spaniards: for to lose the weather gage would make it very difficult to choose their own range. So they seem to have decided to take the best of both worlds – to continue to retain the wind, but, by keeping very close to the Armada, to try, at the last moment, to edge round its flank (especially its left flank) in order to keep themselves between the Spaniards and Spithead.

But though the English ships sailed so well, the English sailing tactics and fleet organization were still extremely rudimentary. It had only been on the preceding day, for instance, that Howard had

67

divided his clumsy array of nearly 200 ships into squadrons at all. Now there were four of them. Howard himself, of course, took one, and, as befitted the Admiral, he lay as near the centre of the English fleet as he could get. His Vice-Admiral, Sir Francis Drake, would, by the usage of that time, have command of the Vanguard, which would always be on the extreme right of the battle. John Hawkins was the Rear-Admiral and Third-in-Command, and – since there was present another flag officer who was junior to him – he must have the squadron between the Commander-in-Chief and the Vice-Admiral. The fourth – and junior – Squadron Commander was Martin Frobisher, whose place, as junior, was on the rear (in this case the port) wing. He was therefore nearest to the island. And in fact it was Frobisher who, if anyone was to do it, was the one to edge round the port wing of the Armada, and take up a position which would prevent it from reaching Spithead. Anyway, whether this was the fore-ordained scheme or not, this is what he did. He was a fine seaman, and one, moreover, willing to take all risks.

So, early in the morning, while the ordinary sou-westerly Channel wind was blowing, he edged inshore, boldly if not recklessly, so as to pass inside the Armada's left wing. But, having proceeded for some distance, he found himself in a very awkward predicament; for by now most of the Spaniards were to windward of him. Then, to add to his troubles, the westerly breeze died away, and there was Frobisher, almost quite alone, and lying motionless on the water. The Spaniards, who had throughout been complaining that the English would never await their coming, now eagerly closed in upon him, convinced that at last they would get to grips and secure a worthwhile prize. (Incidentally, as always, they were sure that Frobisher's ship was the fleet flagship herself, with the Lord Admiral on board).

Meanwhile – even the enemy admitted it – Frobisher was game. Although (according to one Spanish account) his ship, the *Triumph*, had her stern injured so that she could no longer steer (but this was probably mere wishful thinking), he instantly lowered eleven boats which tried to take her in tow. Sidonia's own flagship and all the galleasses, now (as they thought) about to come into their own, leapt in to the kill. But before they had time to reach her, a tiny flaw of land-wind began to blow from the north-east, and the situation changed in a flash. For all their efforts, both of sail and of oar, and 'certain' (as they said) 'that we would this day succeed in boarding them, which was the only way to victory', they found the *Triumph* leaving them all standing. 'She began to slip away', moaned Sidonia, 'and to leave the boats that were rowing her'. Another Spanish eyewitness said, with growing amazement and envy, 'She got out so swiftly that the galleon *San Juan* and another quick-sailing ship – the speediest vessel in the Armada – although they gave chase, seemed in comparison with her to be standing still.' In the whole fight there is perhaps no better illustration of the vast sailing-superiority which the English enjoyed: for of all our ships, the *Triumph* was the largest, the highest-carged, and the most sluggish sailer of the lot.

We know, then, Frobisher's share in this day's fighting: and Howard's, because we know he went in support of the *Triumph*. Unfortunately, however, we know little else for certain. So far Howard's official narrative helps, but – as usual – it never seems to go beyond what he himself saw from his own deck and through his own eyes. There is complete silence on the English side as to the movements of the other two squadrons – and nearly as complete a silence from Spanish sources. Did they then sit still and twiddle their thumbs while Frobisher and Howard gallantly fought it out? Let us not forget that those two squadrons were commanded by the two foremost seamen and the two hardest hitters of that day. It is indeed impossible to believe that Francis Drake and John Hawkins would so rest upon their laurels. Yet no surviving account has deigned to tell us what they did, not even on the Spanish side. Possibly that side had a good reason to hold its peace, and it was not a particularly honest one. The impression that their writers evidently meant to give is that, after so uncanny an exhibition of mobility, the Duke concluded that he would never catch those elusive but cowardly heretics, whatever he did. So (in his own words) 'He discharged a piece and proceeded on his course, the rest of the Armada following in very good order, the enemy remaining a long way astern.' And the other accounts loyally back him up. 'This being seen by the Duke,' says one, 'and the weather being fair, he proceeded on his journey.'

But this simply begs the question. So far, according to them, they were winning all along the line. The English were on the run. But, if so, the Solent (which we know they wished to enter) lay open before them: that ripe plum, the Island, was waiting to drop into their mouths. And yet, in a fit of pique, because they could not catch the English ships, they sailed clean away, leaving the plums on the tree. Why?

The fact, of course, is that Sidonia was already busy covering up his traces. His master had impressed upon him that he was to turn neither to the right nor to the left, but to plod straight on. Well, he had disobeyed his master – and at the same time failed to secure his objective – for he had certainly failed to secure a footing at Spithead. 'Clearly', he thought, 'any statement of mine will later be taken down and used in evidence against me.' So he made no statement but maintained a masterly silence, deliberately missing out one whole phase of the battle. But still we must ask what happened – why, having reached the eastern extremity of the Island, and having thwarted Frobisher's attempt to push round his left flank – why, in the name of commonsense, did Sidonia not carry on northwards and then westwards, until he had entered Spithead: especially when the wind, veering to the north-east, would most kindly have assisted him in his purpose? The answer must surely be that he did at least begin such a move. Whether he and the rest of his main-battle ever reached the anchorage cannot be determined: but that he started such a movement seems reasonably certain. Before he completed it, however, something must have interrupted him. And what was that? The present author thinks he knows, and will therefore proceed to set out his theory.[1] To his mind it is by far the neatest solution to a difficult question.

Drake, then, commanding the starboard squadron of the English fleet (the southernmost, that is, and the furthest out to sea) took no part in the fighting near the Island, leaving that to the squadrons

---

[1] It should be understood that he is not quite the first to propound it. That was done by Sir Julian Corbett many years ago in his *Drake and the Tudor Navy* (1898).

of Frobisher and Howard. (This is quite in keeping with what we know of Sir Francis and his independent mind. On both the earlier days of the action he had rather tended to go off on his own). Hawkins too, commanding the next squadron to the north, decided to follow Drake in making another attack altogether upon the enemy. The whole campaign abounds with examples of the English leaders taking just such independent action. Indeed the whole structure of Lord Howard's command was very weak indeed – often he made no attempt at all to interfere with what his chief subordinates did. One may even go so far as to say that there *was* no concerted fleet-policy, as laid down by the English Commander-in-Chief.

Working then to seaward, on a sou-westerly course while the wind was still at nor-east, they had made enough sea-room, when the wind veered again to the west or sou-west, to be able to charge full upon the Armada's weather flank simply by steering to the north. At the extreme tip of that Spanish starboard wing, lay the galleon *San Mateo*, one of the most powerful in the whole fleet. (Quite a separate despatch from the Captain of this ship survives, which bears out the whole theory.) Reeling under the blows of Drake and Hawkins, she allowed herself to be pushed away from her covering position so that she was driven in upon the body of unwieldy and poorly armed hulks and transports. These in their turn broke up in considerable disorder and fled away to the north-east. But such a course would drive them headlong, and in a very short time, on to the shoals off Selsey Bill, now known as the Owers Bank. At that moment the situation of both the defenceless hulks and of their covering warships was dangerous in the extreme. Indeed, if left to themselves, they would inevitably have piled up on the shallows, and two-thirds of the Armada would have been written off. From such a fate, however, they were saved by the intervention of the Duke himself. By now he must have been approaching Spithead: certainly he must have passed St Helens. But, warned of the impending calamity to his centre (the hulks) and his rear (the fighting ships which covered them), he could only put out suddenly and sail large (i.e. *away* from Spithead) to their help.

It was by no means the first time that Medina Sidonia had been called upon for heroic exertions in saving his weaker brethren from destruction: and now he succeeded again in doing so. As he made his best speed down-wind, Drake (and probably Hawkins too) saw him coming. Being in hot chase of the hulks, they were now themselves quite near the fatal banks: but neither felt it part of his duty to face the Spanish main battle, as it came down upon them before the wind. They had not done so yet, and they had no intention of doing so now. They therefore broke off the chase and simply stood out to sea again on a southerly course. Then, tacking back to the west, they safely rejoined the other two squadrons of their own fleet. So Sidonia had succeeded in saving his hulks and their escorts: but at what a cost! By the time the Duke had reached his stricken ships, the whole Armada had drifted almost as far as Selsey – miles, that is, to leeward of the Spithead entrance – with a head-wind blowing, moreover, which made it quite impossible to get back. So all chance of landing upon the Island was lost, and there was no longer any possibility of entering Spithead.

Here, suddenly, Sidonia's 'cover story' becomes true again – or at least acquires the semblance of truth. 'He discharged a piece and proceeded on his course' – just as though nothing had happened between the escape of the *Triumph* and this moment. So, very likely Sidonia's master never knew how his servant had tried – and failed – to depart from his instructions. Yet undoubtedly what had happened during that glossed-over interval was the most important thing that had yet befallen the Armada. The Duke reached Calais all right, only to have his worst fears confirmed – the Duke of Parma was *not* ready. So the ships had to drop anchor in a place where there was no anchorage at all. And they had to submit to the danger of attack by fire-ships: which, when they came, though they set no Spanish vessel alight, yet did succeed in doing what the English fleet had hitherto failed to do – to break up once for all the Armada's stubborn formation. In this way it became a comparatively easy prey to the English ships at the Battle of Gravelines. It is certain that this action was 'the beginning of the end' because, after it, the Duke was committed to try and return to Spain by the north-about route round Scotland. But what a great Englishman was later to call 'the end of the beginning' was when Sidonia tried, and failed, to anchor in Spithead.

### c. *Actions Since 1588*

Since that July day, 384 years ago, only once again has there been fighting in Spithead itself. This time it was no foreign foe who invaded it. But fighting it was none the less, and Englishmen were now attacking Englishmen. In 1642, the nation was busy taking sides in what was to be the great Civil War. In that desperate quarrel the role of the Navy was a leading one, though it is little known. In fact it can be argued that it was the Navy's action, more than any other one thing, which decided the whole issue. In a word Parliament contrived to win over the King's Ships to its side, and Spithead was one of the scenes of this most vital success. In the process, blood was shed – very little of it, it is true – but the tragedy of it was that it was English blood spilled by Englishmen.

Hitherto, royal ships were built and maintained from the King's own revenue, but under James I the royal finances were in a parlous state, his ships were neglected, and pirates began to infest the Channel again. Charles I tried to restore order – indeed to form a permanent naval force rather than a temporary one raised in moments of crisis – by levying Ship Money from all over England. The nation will benefit from a fleet, he said, so let the nation pay. This argument stuck in few people's throats. What did cause trouble was Charles's other formula – nation pays, King controls – at which wide demand arose for Parliamentary control. With his Ship Money, Charles built a fleet – the first to be paid for by the nation – and began to clear up the Channel. But the cash was not spent in the wisest way. The King, a lover of ships and of art, laid out too much on unnecessarily lavish vessels – the great gilded stern of the *Sovereign of the Seas*, for instance, cost him thousands. As a result he did not have enough left over to pay his seamen or even to feed and clothe them properly.

Disaffection spread. Of the officers, a few were Puritans or Parliamentarians for personal reasons; but most of them when reduced to selling the masts and spars out of their ships to keep

73

their men fed, simply felt that the existing state of things was not good enough. The seamen likewise had few political ideas, and were merely concerned with bettering the appalling conditions in which they served. When Parliament offered higher wages – 19s a month for seamen instead of the theoretical but unpaid 15s – both officers and men jumped at it. Charles regarded their action as mutiny: 'How is it', he mourned, 'that I have lost the hearts of these water rats?' Yet they were not traitors, merely human beings; not so much mutineers as demonstrators against the King's methods; with no thought of getting rid of the King, but willing to serve him while being managed by Parliament.

The crux came in 1642, when the Earl of Warwick was appointed Admiral of the Fleet by Parliament, against the King's wishes. The fleet in the Thames preferred to serve him rather than any King's nominee, and offered its services to Parliament. Only five Captains felt the conflict of loyalties strongly enough to refuse to come over. The fleet at Spithead, however, did not move so fast. When in August the Governor of Portsmouth, Sir George Goring, suddenly declared for the King, Warwick, who was quick to realize to the full the importance of the port to Parliament, instantly dispatched the robustly Puritan Captain Richard Swanley in the *Charles*, 44 guns, to deal with the ships in the harbour and those lying at Spithead. With great determination and dispatch Swanley sent his lieutenant, Brown Bushell, in boats to attack the King's Ship *Henrietta* which was acting as guard-ship in the harbour mouth. So unexpected was the assault that the *Henrietta*'s crew put up very little fight before surrendering. Some days later Bushell, with some seamen from his ship, equally suddenly surprised that very strong post, Southsea Castle, by swimming the moat in the early hours and scaling the ramparts to call upon the Royalist Commander to surrender. That worthy, who was just recovering from a drunken revelry, found he had lost the whole castle – much the strongest fortification in the neighbourhood – before he could recover his wits. He considered himself the victim of a burglarious break-in and an exceedingly ungentlemanly intrusion. The next day the Roundheads turned the guns of the castle on the town and demanded its surrender. Captain Bushell's first shot provoked such

a thunderous reply that he almost abandoned his capture. None
the less, he held on, and his success caused many seamen and
Royalist troops to change allegiance. Colonel Goring had to
surrender the town, but he threatened to destroy it by detonating
the magazine in the Square Tower at the bottom of the High
Street. His reckless courage and determination were known, and
he was believed. So he and his soldiers were allowed to march out
and away with all the honours of war – flags flying, drums beating,
and bearing weapons. And he had the last word. As he left he took
the key of the Landport Gate and tossed it into the sea (whence it
was almost miraculously recovered nearly three hundred years
later). The Parliamentarians marched in and the Earl of Warwick
took possession of the town, the harbour and the ships. Then
Swanley, boldly and on his own initiative, attacked the Isle of
Wight and, with almost equal ease, overran it. Finally Carisbrooke
Castle, though strongly held for the King, surrendered in panic
when Swanley appeared before it with a handful of sailors. Thus
the whole vital area, ships and all, fell into the lap of Parliament, and
remained so throughout the first (and most important) Civil War.

Since 1642 there have been no more actions of any sort in or
close to Spithead against either foreigners or anyone else, with the
exception of aerial warfare waged over its waters. The reason for
this is not far to seek. Ever since then, a united England has been
– more or less – a sea-power to be reckoned with: sufficiently so,
anyway, to prevent foreigners from penetrating into the fastnesses
of her principal naval base, or even to the Island that covers it.
And there have been no more civil wars. Yet, naturally, engage-
ments have taken place in the Channel outside it: and, several
times, our enemies have contemplated attacks, especially upon the
Isle of Wight. The first full-scale fighting that took place near it
occurred during our first encounter with the Dutch Republic in
1652–3. Once, in the first year of the war, the great Martin Tromp
defeated our naval forces – under Robert Blake – off Dungeness to
the east, and had the Channel at his mercy for several months; so
that, had such been his objective, he could have entered Spithead
or made an attack upon the Island. But the Dutch used the English
Channel for a very different purpose – as the highway to and from

75

Holland for their extensive trade. So, though on this occasion Tromp hoisted a broom at his mast-head, meaning vaingloriously to imply that the Channel was his by right and that he would sweep up every English ship which tried to interfere with him, it never occurred to him to occupy any part of England at all. Indeed for that purpose the Dutch never had sufficient man-power to interfere with us. And, early in the following year, it was too late. The opportunity such as it was had gone.

By the spring of 1653, Blake was ready for him again, and he attacked fiercely and successfully a large convoy of merchantmen which Tromp was trying to pass up the Channel. The battle that followed was joined off Portland Bill, and from there a running fight raged right up the Channel almost to the entrance to the Dutch ports, with Blake inflicting enormous losses to the Dutch trade, her very life-blood. The second day's fighting took place off the Island, and here – though he successfully continued the chase – Blake was grievously wounded, and was brought ashore, across Spithead to Portsmouth, more dead than alive: and here he lay for a long time recovering from his injury. Incidentally it was from Portsmouth that he wrote his epoch-making report to his masters, the Commonwealth Government, which resulted in his being given the right to hold courts martial at sea – a privilege no Commander-in-Chief had ever had entrusted to him before. This decision of headquarters gave an immense accession of power to the man in control of our fleets at sea: which, for the first time indeed, turned General Blake into *Admiral* Blake. For that very concession of the power to punish delinquents at sea had conferred upon the Commander of fleets just one important 'droit of Admiralty', so that, thereafter and for ever more, he assumed the *title* of Admiral.

Thirty-six years later we were at war with France again, in that conflict known as the War of the English Succession which put William of Orange upon the throne of England. Then – in 1690 – the newly built navy of France, under their renowned Admiral, the Comte de Tourville, contrived to inflict a heavy defeat upon the English fleet under Arthur Herbert, Earl of Torrington. The action took place this time off Beachy Head, and Torrington as a result withdrew his ships into the Thames, leaving the whole Channel at

Tourville's mercy. There can be no doubt that, had the French wished it, they could have landed on the Island of Wight, having (unlike the Dutch) the necessary troops to seize and hold it. But Tourville, too, lost his opportunity, though he did think of making such a landing. All he did do was to attack and burn the fishing village of Teignmouth on the Devon coast, and then somewhat ingloriously went home. But meanwhile, William's Government (which had rather unwisely dispersed the English Channel fleet) collected it together again, and soon re-established our by now customary command of our home waters.

Much the same sequence of events occurred again in 1779, when we were once more fighting against France, now allied with our rebellious colonies in the War of American Independence. This time, disastrous political internal quarrels in Britain kept most of our best naval commanders on shore, and an immense combined fleet of France and Spain under Admiral Conflans invaded the Channel, threatening the shores of the South of England. Our fleet, inferior in its numbers and commanded by an elderly dug-out, gave ground before it. But this time the Admiral, Sir Charles Hardy, did not retreat right out of the Channel, but by clever manoeuvring, when he came opposite the Island, turned into Spithead, and anchored there. Again Conflans considered attacking the Isle of Wight, but again thought better of it: and with reason, because the situation in 1779 was nothing like so favourable to him as it had been to Tourville in 1690. For, then, the nearest British fleet had been well over one hundred miles away – up the Thames. But, now, a hostile squadron – smaller than his own, it is true, but very much in being – lay close at hand, and all ready to leap upon him if he made any attempt on the Island. So he refrained, and weakly did nothing at all until a stupid quarrel broke out between the French and Spanish commanders, when the whole expedition tamely took itself off to its respective home ports.

In the early nineteenth century when Napoleon tried to invade England, his plan – a grandiose and rather ineffective one – was based upon Boulogne and the Narrow Seas, and not on the Island and Spithead – which did not come into the picture at all. Since then, almost to the present day, no enemy has fixed his envious eyes upon out shores. But in the 1850s and 1860s we imagined that Emperor Napoleon III's eyes were envious. In 1851, such was our suspicion of the last of the Bonapartes that a Royal Commission was appointed to report on the defences of Great Britain in general and of Portsmouth in particular. We seemed to have forgotten our first-line bulwark, the Navy (which was indeed, for the moment, in a very odd state of flux). So five forts were ordered to protrude from the waves of Spithead. Four of them were actually built, and stand to this day; one on the Horse and Dean Sand, another on No Man's Land, the third on the Spit Sand, and the last, St Helens, upon a shoal at the entrance to Brading Harbour. In addition, along the brow of Portsdown Hill an elaborate semi-circle of forts was erected to defend Spithead and the town from the landward side. They were the result of pure panic – Palmerston's, Parliament's and the People's – but they were there to defend the naval base without which the fleet could not operate for long. They really did form the *ne plus ultra* of defence – a defence that by its impregnability avoids the need to defend itself – and deserved more than the common nickname 'Palmerston's Follies'.

Even in 1940, when Hitler for a while really intended invasion, Portsmouth and Spithead were by no means in the front line. The German invasion-plan 'Sea-Lion' envisaged a number of landings from Folkestone in the east to Beachy Head in the west, with a follow-up attack between Brighton and Arundel. Portsmouth was scheduled to fall only just before what they called 'The First Objective' was reached – at the most optimistic estimate, a full week after the first landing. No doubt this late date in the programme was due to the anticipated difficulty of the attack on the Portsmouth defences. But – since all was to depend upon the Luftwaffe's knocking out the R.A.F. – the whole scheme was, and remained, problematical. In fact, it never happened at all – 'the Few' were *not* knocked out. Later in the same year, it is true, the Luftwaffe took its revenge upon Portsmouth by bombing not only the Dockyard (which was a legitimate target) but also the civilian population (which was not). So, for years afterwards, the town showed her war-wounds; but not Spithead which, being strictly fluid, showed no such scars.

# Chapter IV

# ACCIDENTS IN OR
# NEAR SPITHEAD

From Action we pass to Accident. Indeed in any place where so many ships are accustomed to pass so long a time, accidents are bound to happen: they are inherent in the very trade and profession of the seaman.

'Oh Eternal Lord God,' says the old Naval Prayer, 'who alone spreadest out the heavens, and rulest the raging of the sea: Who hast compassed the waters with bounds until day and night come to an end; be pleased to receive into thy Almighty and most gracious protection the persons of us thy servants, and the Fleet in which we serve. Preserve us from the dangers of the sea and the violence of the enemy. . . .'

These are indeed the perils which beset all mariners – the dangers of the sea and the violence of the enemy. And in all ages, save perhaps the most modern ones, it is certain that the dangers of the sea have been the seaman's chief peril. This has been true of all waters, wherever they lie, but it is especially true of a great anchorage like Spithead. Here, as these pages have shown, the violence of the enemy has in recent times taken hardly any toll at all. Between the Middle Ages and the Second World War our enemies have never contrived to destroy any of our ships lying in it, though they have, of course, destroyed a number of their individual companies. And, in Spithead at any rate, even the dangers of the sea have taken their toll comparatively seldom because, full and by, its waters are remarkably friendly to mariners.

Nevertheless the perils that threaten all ships are manifold. Mere destruction from violent seas is only one of them, and, in sheltered waters, by no means the most perilous or the commonest. In the list of accidents chronicled here, there is perhaps only one where a British ship has come to its end from this cause and no other. In all other cases – and the list is in all conscience tragic enough – the causes of disaster have been different. Three of the worst, involving the saddest loss of human life, have been due to faulty construction in the ships themselves – one (the best remembered of them all) the result of near-criminal administrative neglect. Two more were caused by that worst of all enemies to ships of war – and especially in the days of wooden ships – fire. The loss of two more was due to explosions of that highly dangerous material, perforce carried on board all fighting ships – gunpowder. And there were doubtless other ships, mainly from the earliest days, whose fate – and even whose names – are lost in the mists of the past. Here are chronicled only such whose names and whose fates are known – and the present author is fain to admit that some even of these have escaped his vigilance.

The earliest known example of disaster to a ship of the Navy Royal in or near Spithead has already been mentioned,[1] but was not fully dealt with at that point. This was the *Mary Rose*, sunk perhaps in the presence of an enemy fleet, yet certainly not *by* that enemy. She was named after Mary Tudor, the sister of Henry VIII. She carried in all eighty-five guns, and though some of them were very small, some also were really large. She was perhaps the best sailer, the most weatherly, of all the King's Ships. Though built in 1509, she had been rebuilt and brought up to date in 1536. She carried, in addition to her Captain, Sir George Carew, some 400 men, of whom 200 were soldiers, 180 mariners and 20 gunners.

At some moment in the fight – but which is not clear – she was off the Solent shore of the Isle of Wight, and was, probably, in the act of putting about, to regain her anchorage under Southsea Castle. As she turned, she naturally heeled over a little, with the result that her lower-deck gunports dipped into the sea. She instantly filled and sank. All, or practically all, of her men were lost.

There is still some mystery about the mishap. Sir Walter Raleigh

[1] See page 61.

7. Spit Sand Fort from Spithead. The Harbour entrance lies to its right

8. General Pasley's divers clearing the wreck of the *Royal George*, 1844. Ryde and its pier lie beyond

9. The explosion of the *Boyne*, 1795;
'An opaque white cloud like a round
cap'. Southsea Castle is on the left

10. Figurehead of the *Eurydice*
(minus the telescope)

(not quite a contemporary) says that this was the case, adding that her lower ports were only sixteen inches above the waterline. But this seems almost impossible. Ports for the big guns had been cut in the lower decks of ships for at least fifty years, and the *Mary Rose* had been brought up to date only nine years before. But, even if Sir Walter is right, his explanation of itself fails to explain. If there was only this sixteen-inch margin of safety, the officers must have known about it, and would therefore have taken great pains to see that the ports were shut down whenever there was any danger of the water coming in. Such danger, of course, would always be present when the ship went about suddenly: for that would give her a list. Probably, then, the trouble lay in something additional to the over-low port holes. And what it was is indirectly revealed by the researches of Michael Oppenheim,[1] who, writing in 1896, poured scorn on the 'low-port' theory, and advanced another reason altogether. He quotes the evidence of the chronicler Stow, who points out that the discipline on board the ship was shocking. And the biographer of Sir Peter Carew, brother of the lost Captain,[2] adds his testimony to what Stow had to say, which seems conclusive. Sir Peter, referring to the accident in which his brother lost his life, writes,

> he had a sort of knaves whom he could not rule, [who] refusing to do that which they should do were careless to do that which was most needful and necessary, and . . . so contending in envy, perished in frowardness.

Evidently, then, Raleigh, Stow and Peter Carew may all have been right – if, that is, the Captain's orders (to close ports on turning) had been deliberately disobeyed by a bloody-minded crew, perhaps the worse for drink: with the result that the ship flooded quickly, drowning them all.

On almost the very day that she was lost, Henry, we are told, ordered his Italian engineers to attempt her recovery, and by all accounts they were quite near to success. But not quite: the

---

[1] M. Oppenheim, *Administration of the Royal Navy*, p. 66.
[2] R. Hooker, *Life of Sir Peter Carew*, pp. 34-5.

technical difficulties of sixteenth-century ship salvage were just too great – though the Italians did contrive to consume twenty-two tuns of beer in the process, and took some £500 in wages for their efforts.

For nearly 300 years she lay where she had sunk. Then in the 1830s divers went down, discovered the location of the wreck, and succeeded in retrieving some of her guns. This attempt revealed a most interesting fact, that at the moment of her loss she was in the very middle of a major rearmament. Many of the pieces recovered can still be seen in the Rotunda at Woolwich and at the National Maritime Museum at Greenwich. Some of them were of the crudest medieval type – 'built-up', trunnionless guns composed of bars of forged iron bound together by bands of metal sweated on to them. On the other hand, some – the new armament – were cast-iron pieces made in a mould, and reinforced at the breech: practically identical in fact with the guns which were to win the Battle of Trafalgar 260 years later.

The site of the wreck was lost again until 1969, when with the aid of aqualungs, echo-sounding gear and the latest electronic equipment, the *Mary Rose* was located by Alexander McKee of the British Sub-Aqua Club. Her identity was proved by the recovery of one of her unique welded guns in very fine condition. The wreck lies some thirty feet below the bottom of Spithead, in mud which has preserved the lower parts in an iron-like hardness. A submarine survey is being made by skin-divers, and there are hopes of her being raised to the surface in the manner of the *Vasa*. It is an exciting thought: to be able to view again a ship nearly a century older than that Swedish treasure.

The loss of the *Mary Rose* was, however one looks at it, a stark tragedy. The next accident to be reported was not nearly so serious, and it even had its mildly humorous side. It was the only accident described here which did not prove fatal to a gallant ship. In January 1673, while the Third Dutch War was still on, one of the finest third-rates in the Navy, the *Resolution*, was commissioned at Portsmouth, and then went out to Spithead preparatory to joining the fleet. But just before she sailed, an odd accident happened to her which very nearly proved her last. On her last night in the anchorage, while her Captain was on shore getting his final instructions, one of her Yeomen of the Powder Room somehow got it into his head that a powder chest standing outside the forward magazine was empty. Indeed, he was so sure of it that, breaking all the rules, he went down to examine it with a lighted and exposed candle in his hand. (The usual procedure was, of course, far otherwise. The precautions taken over such an inflammable thing as powder in a wooden ship were quite impressive. No one ever took a naked light anywhere near the stuff. Instead, donning felt slippers, the Gunner or one of his Yeomen entered the powder magazine in darkness, relying for his illumination upon a lantern which burned outside the room, in a special compartment with a thick talc window (which was never opened) letting on to the powder room.)

This time, however, the Yeoman confidently descended into the hold, naked candle in hand. He bent over the chest, and his light revealed that it was at least not full to the brim: which, in its turn, seemed to confirm his belief that it was empty. But – alas for the poor Yeoman! – while he was in the very act of peering in, the ship's cat, intent upon catching a well-nourished rat, collided with his legs so unexpectedly that in his surprise he let go of his candle. It fell, still alight, into the chest which, though not full (since that very morning the Gunner had been making up cartridges out of its contents) was yet about a quarter full. The powder naturally went up, igniting with its flash the nearest cartridge which the Gunner had left on the floor of the magazine. This ignited the nearest but one, then the nearest but two, and so on. It looked, in short, as though the whole fore-magazine must go up, in which case the ship must be lost.

The series of explosions, heard from above, so frightened the ship's company that they all leapt overboard into the anchorage – all, that is, save the Lieutenant, temporarily in charge of the ship, and two hands to whom at that moment he chanced to be giving orders. The first-named – an intrepid officer – now lost no time in going down the hatch into the forward hold, accompanied by his two trusties. The original explosion had blown open the door of the Beer Room, and the combined exertions of the three of them enabled them to drag out a very large and full hogshead. This they rolled to the door of the fore-magazine, stove its head in, and flooded the compartment with beer. And this unusual use of the ship's beverage did the trick. The explosion, and the resultant fire which was just taking hold, were mercifully quenched in the flood, and the *Resolution* was saved.

The Yeoman of the Powder Room was not court martialled for his very heinous crime in jeopardizing the ship: he was not even blown up by the Captain when he returned. Still, he *was* blown up by the initial explosion, and so passed beyond the reach of either Captain or Admiralty. He was the only fatal casualty on board.

Towards the end of the War of the Spanish Succession, Admiral Sir Hovenden Walker was sent over to the east coast of North America, carrying the cream of Marlborough's army with him, with orders to make his way up the St Lawrence River and capture Quebec from the French. He failed rather egregiously, and returned under a cloud to England, dropping anchor at Spithead on October 9, 1711. Six days later his flagship, the seventy-gun *Edgar*, exploded suddenly, fatally and inexplicably. No one knows to this day what happened or why it happened – whether perhaps some infatuated Yeoman of the Powder Room tried once too often to repeat the experiment of the *Resolution* – because everybody on board, nearly 400 of them, perished. The whole complement of the *Edgar* was not lost, however. Every officer was saved, being in fact absent from the ship – they were all on shore at Portsmouth at the time. It is tempting to suppose that, in the absence of the cats, the mice were frolicking, and it may well be so, though if the warrant officers were still on board it should not have happened.

But then another proverb leaps to mind – 'It's an ill wind that blows nobody any good'. Though Walker himself suffered no hurt from the explosion, all his papers, public and private alike, were still on board and went up with the ship. He was very lucky, because a court martial was impending, as a result of which he would, beyond all doubt, have been struck off the flag-list. The Admiralty, however, had the humanity to declare that the destruction of the evidence made a prosecution impossible just then. Indeed they even gave him another command, but recalled him from it after a year, inviting him to give an account of the Quebec affair from memory. He replied that he could not do so; whereupon he was dismissed from the service without a pension. This seems a little harsh, but there are some reasons for thinking that this severity was not due to anything he had done amiss in America, but to a suspicion that he was a Jacobite. There has never been any suspicion, though, that he engineered the explosion in the *Edgar*. He was hardly subtle enough for that.

In 1844, Major-General C. W. Pasley, Royal Engineers, discovered the wreck: or, to be more strictly accurate, one-third of the wreck. It seems that, in 1711, both her fore- and her after-magazines had gone up, breaking her into three parts and disintegrating the fore- and the after-parts. And now, 133 years later, Pasley's diver, on a day when the water was exceptionally clear, found himself gazing at the ship's central section, standing on an even keel thirteen-and-a-half feet above the level of the sea bottom with all the guns which properly belonged to that section still in their original positions. They were recovered, but not by dragging them out through the ports. They were lifted straight up, the woodwork of the decks giving no resistance at all to their passage.

The next two accidents occurred during the War of American Independence: the first, a comparatively minor one, took place near the beginning of it; the second almost at the end of it, and a most disgraceful one too.

On July 5, 1776, the *Marlborough*, a 74-gun ship, blew up in Spithead, killing thirty of her company and grievously maiming many others. Neither the cause of the accident nor any details of it are known.

The other accident was a calamity of the first order, the most dramatic and pathetic in all Spithead's long history, and perhaps the best known accident to a British man-of-war that has ever happened. The *Royal George* was a first-rate of 100 guns, and she carried at the time the flag of that great officer, Rear-Admiral Richard Kempenfelt. She was by no means a new ship and for a long time it had been known to most officers, executive and dock-yard alike, that she was in need of a major refit. But, with practically all the maritime nations at war against us, no one was very

85

willing to have her laid up in dock. The Admiralty – at that time corrupt through and through – refused to listen to what the experts had to say. So she was retained in active commission.

On August 29, 1782, the great ship lay in Spithead, and was being slightly careened to correct some underwater defects. With her known weakness, she should of course have been taken into dock, though the projected repair was quite a minor one. But no one troubled to do that. Instead, they gave her what in those days was called a 'parliamentary heel'. The method adopted was the normal one of transferring a number of her guns from one side of the deck to the other, in order to give her the necessary cant to expose some of her underwater timbers. The amount of heel required for the work was so slight that everyone, officers and men alike, were getting on with their usual chores. At this time, over and above the usual ship's company, there were on board a great number of wives and children of the crew, taking this opportunity of visiting their menfolk. Suddenly a loud crack was heard, and she sank like a stone. There was no time for much rescue work, and more than 1,000 souls went down with her, including the wise and gallant Kempenfelt, who was quietly writing in his cabin.

Several accounts are extant about what happened during that tragic split second. A seaman called Henry Bishop

> Saw the port-side gun-ports go dark, as they went below the sea, cutting off the light: then the inrush of water pushed him up a hatchway in which he met a starboard-side gun on its way down: with three fingers broken by the collision, he burst to the surface and was taken up by a boat.[1]

Another man, James Ingram, tried to run his gun back into its former position, but the ship heeled so quickly that the gun took charge. Then Ingram, in self-preservation, made a leap for the gun-port and contrived to squeeze through it, emerging not, as one usually would, over the water, but straight up in the air, since the ship now lay on her beam-ends with her starboard side just above

[1] Alexander McKee, *History under the Sea*, pp. 31–2.

86

the water. He too was picked up. These were two of the few lucky ones.

Everyone knows the lament of the poet William Cowper – 'Toll for the brave – the brave that are no more!' But Cowper was told the official story which Britons were expected to believe, and which most people not in the know did believe. 'A land-breeze shook the shrouds', he sang, 'and she was overset.' This was, in fact, nonsense. Had there been any breeze at all worth mentioning, the men's families would not have been on board. 'Weigh the vessel up!' he urged, but the Government, who knew what would be found if they did raise her, were naturally most reluctant to try. 'Her timbers yet are sound,' he concluded, 'and she may float again.' But here he was terribly mistaken – her timbers were so very far from sound that a great piece of her rotten bottom had simply fallen out. The evidence at the court of inquiry of Admiral Milbanke and Captain John Jervis (afterwards Earl St Vincent) was quite conclusive on this point. She was unseaworthy through and through.

Though the Admiralty's attempts to raise her were only make-believe, something had to be done about her, because she was a danger to all shipping using the anchorage. Eight years later her mizzen mast still protruded from the water to mark where she lay.[1] There is no hope whatever, now, that 'she will float again'. In the 1840s, the Royal Engineers (Plate 8), in a practice exercise, went over the whole of Spithead anchorage with high explosives sweeping for wrecks: and, among others, removed all that was left of the ship.

Why did the old ship pack up on that particular August day? We shall never know, but we are entitled to make an intelligent guess. It is based upon a proverb – 'It's the last straw that breaks the camel's back'. Let us suppose that the *Royal George's* frame was already overstrained to the very point of collapsing; and that, on that day, two last straws were added, each of them in itself very

---

[1] See *Dillon's Narrative* (Navy Records Society, 1953), vol. i, pp. 13–14. It is significant to find that he, like Cowper, still attributes her loss to the wrong cause. Ingram's narrative was used almost verbatim for Chapter 19 of Marryat's *Poor Jack*.

light. There was first the undoubted fact that she was carrying at the moment a larger and therefore heavier crowd of people than usual – instead of her ordinary complement of 800 she had over 1,000 on board. Then, on top of this, came the 'parliamentary heel' – perfectly safe in a normally sound ship, but highly hazardous in one whose bottom was on the point of giving out anyway. The shifting of the guns to heel her over, slight as it was, would set the whole cranky concern in motion: might well, in fact, be the last straw of the proverb.

During the Revolutionary War against France (1793–1801) the British Navy grew to an unprecedented size, so that Portsmouth Harbour and Spithead were fuller of all kinds of shipping than ever before. There was then room for accidents above the average both in number and importance.

In August 1794, after Lord Howe's return from the Battle of the Glorious First of June, one of his prizes, the third-rate ship *Impétueux*, was accidentally lost in Portsmouth Harbour in unusual circumstances. The cause of the trouble was that on the way to Portsmouth after the battle some hidden smouldering timber in her shot-riddled sides burst into flames and, as was usual when in hazard from fire, the magazines were flooded (a precaution still used). When she was safely on moorings in Portsmouth Harbour a party was sent from the guard-ship to empty the magazine. They had wooden buckets and wooden bailers and they lit their way between decks with sealed safety lanterns. It was a messy, sloppy, business, carrying the buckets of gunpowder slush from the magazine to the ship's side, and much was spilt. Eventually one man's lamp went out and he rashly, in defiance of all orders and regulations, opened the lamp and relit it. Aware of his sin and justifiably nervous, as well as lazy, he dropped the lantern on the deck where the damp powder ignited and behaved as a slow fuse. The magazines did not explode, but the whole ship took fire and burnt right down to the waterline before sinking.

Another prize taken in the battle was the French frigate *Amérique*. This ship was built during the War of Independence as the *America*. After the war, the United States presented her to her ally France as a token of gratitude. Following the careless loss of the *Impétueux*, the British decided to rename the *Amérique* as the *Impétueux*. It is unlikely that this was merely an attempt to cover up the destruction of the latter, since the *Amérique* was a most distinctive vessel. People came to Portsmouth from miles away to look at her, for she was reputed to have the most beautiful 'gingerbread' work on her stern yet seen in this harbour.

On May 1, 1795, however, a much worse disaster happened out in the roads to a 98-gun ship, the *Boyne*, which had been carrying the flag of Vice-Admiral Sir John Jervis. She was lying with her consorts in the anchorage when, at eleven o'clock in the morning, it was suddenly noticed by all the other ships of the squadron that she was on fire. The flames spread so rapidly that, within half an hour, in spite of all the exertions of her officers and men, she was ablaze from stem to stern. Every ship instantly sent out all available boats to her assistance, and all but eleven seamen out of her very large crew were picked up. All the vessels which were to leeward of her, and therefore in danger of taking fire themselves, were ordered to get under way and did so, in spite of the fact that both wind and tide were against them. They made their way to St Helens, and returned only when the danger was over.

Rescue work, however, was hazardous, because all the *Boyne*'s guns (as customary in wartime, even in harbour) were fully loaded; and as they became red-hot, they discharged their roundshot indiscriminately among the shipping that lay around. Thus two of the crew of the great first-rate, the *Queen Charlotte* (so soon to suffer the same fate in the Mediterranean), were killed by this unintentional fire, and a third was badly wounded. Some of the shots even reached the shore in Stokes Bay to the west of Gosport, while a number of sheep, browsing innocently on Southsea Common, were slaughtered. After a while her cables burnt through and parted, and she began to drift slowly eastwards, grounding at last on the Spit Sand opposite Southsea Castle, where she continued to burn until six o'clock. Then the flames reached her fore-magazine, far below the waterline, and the whole ship went up with an appalling roar. Captain Edward Brenton, the naval historian, was an eye-witness of the whole incident, and has left a vivid description of the scene:

The blowing up of her fore-magazine offered one of the most magnificent sights that can be conceived: the afternoon was perfectly calm and the sky clear: the flames which darted from her in a perpendicular column of great height was terminated by an opaque white cloud like a round cap, while the air was filled with fragments of wreck in every direction.[1]

To this description, the rival historian William James (who quotes the passage from Brenton) adds that 'the stump of the foremast was seen far above the smoke, descending into the water'.

She was, of course, burnt out right down to the waterline, and was not worth retrieving. The future victor of Cape St Vincent was not on board at the time. He was attending a court martial which was sitting at Portsmouth. All his personal possessions and all his papers were totally lost.

Naturally, a court of inquiry was held upon the disaster. Its findings, however, were by no means conclusive. Two rival explanations held the field – the first much the more likely, the second much the more picturesque. Brenton himself maintained that the overheating of the funnel of the wardroom stove, which passed through the deck, ignited the Admiral's cabin above it. But James gives quite another reason for the conflagration:

A part of the lighted paper from the cartridges of the marines, who were exercising and firing on the windward side of the poop, flew through the quarter-gallery to the Admiral's cabin, and communicated with the papers and other inflammable materials [lying there].[2]

James and Brenton were bitter enemies who delighted in scoring each other off. Here James condescends to borrow from Brenton who, after all, had been an eyewitness of the atomic mushroom. When it comes to reciting causes, however, he puts his

[1] Edward Brenton, *Naval History of Great Britain*, vol. i, p. 228. An aquatint of the explosion survives (Plate 9). To twentieth-century eyes it looks just like an atomic explosion.
[2] William James, *Naval History of Great Britain*, vol. i, p. 286.

own theory first – the one about the marines – adding Brenton's almost as an afterthought, as though to say, 'Poor boob! He *would* think that!' Usually, when they contradict each other, James is probably in the right: but this time he is probably in the wrong. After all, heated flues are common causes of fires even now. But burning papers floating through windows from marines' muskets must be quite rare. Perhaps, however, the reason for the conflagration does not greatly matter: what is certain is that a fine ship was no more. The site is still marked by the Boyne Buoy. In 1832, the inventor of the modern diving suit, Charles Dean, paid a short underwater visit to the ship. He had not much time in which to make an exhaustive search, but he did have time to retrieve three bottles of wine, two of which he presented to his patron, King William IV. Whether the wine was still drinkable after its submersion of thirty-seven years we are not told.

Rather more than four years later another ship, nearly as big as the *Boyne*, came to grief in the neighbourhood of Spithead, though not quite in it. She was the 90-gun *Impregnable*, commanded by Captain Jonathan Faulknor, and was returning home on October 19, 1799, at the end of a long commission abroad. The season was getting late for ships of this size still to be at sea, and no doubt her officers were anxious to make the anchorage at the earliest possible moment. The weather, it seems, was calm and misty. Clearly her Master was in a hurry, and was trying to make Spithead that night. But he was out in his reckoning – no unusual event in foggy weather – and in coming in from the east, instead of hitting the channel up Spithead, he took the ship too far to the north, and far too early. The result was that he ran her aground under press of canvas on the Poles shoal off Chichester Harbour. She struck so hard that, before anything could be done about it, she had seven feet of water in her hold. Instantly her masts and yards were cut away, but it was too late. Though all possible assistance was rendered by other ships and from the shore, she was irretrievably lost, and had to be abandoned. Almost all the crew were rescued, but the wreck had to be written off as a total loss, the remains being sold out of the service for a mere song.

Though Jonathan Faulknor, as Captain of the ship, was of

course ultimately responsible for her loss, he seems to have had no difficulty in persuading the court of inquiry held upon her that the Master, and not himself, was responsible: and – perhaps surprisingly – he left the court without even a smear against his name. This could hardly happen now. But two things ought to be remembered. First, wooden sailing ships, even the grandest of them, cost exceedingly little compared with the steel leviathans of the twentieth century, and we had so many of them that one was – relatively – expendable. Secondly, and probably much more important – Faulknor's father (also Jonathan) had died, a full Admiral, only very recently, and the whole clan had great naval 'interest'. He was given another ship at once, and within five years was promoted to flag rank.

This was a case comparatively rare in the annals of the Royal Navy – one of rather culpable negligence on the part of the man responsible for the navigation of the ship. Normally Masters R.N. were among the steadiest people in the Service, and the least prone to fall into errors of judgement, still less of carelessness. But clearly this one had. In his eagerness to reach home that night, he had taken the altogether unwarranted risk which ended so disastrously. The present author has not been able to discover his fate: but, unless he too had 'interest' (which is, to say the least, doubtful), his Service future cannot have been hopeful.

November 9, 1799 (three weeks later), was not a lucky day for local shipping; for on that day two merchantmen in the harbour caught fire, and so did H.M.S. *Prince Frederick*, a 64-gun ship at anchor in Spithead. Were these mishaps, by any chance, the result of arson? There is no evidence of this; but some spark of the great mutinies of only two years before may still have been smouldering.

By contrast with the Revolutionary War, the even larger Napoleonic War of 1803–14, with an even larger navy in commission, passed relatively uneventfully in Spithead insofar as accidents were concerned. The only one known to the author was the old *Vigilant*, 64, a prison-ship lying in the roads, which one April day quietly sank at her moorings. They raised her up, and put her into dock. But what happened to her prisoners when she went down is not mentioned by anyone.

A most melancholy form of accident is when anything goes wrong with a training ship. Such a tragedy occurred on March 24, 1878. The *Eurydice* was a wooden sailing frigate which was being used to take parties of young naval seamen for long cruises in foreign waters. She was now returning to Portsmouth after one such trip. All was in order: there was no reason at all to anticipate trouble. On the 23rd she had rounded the eastern point of the Isle of Wight, and her officers confidently expected to reach Spithead next day. When the 24th dawned, the *Eurydice* was sighted by coastguards on the Island making fine progress to the northward under full sail. The day was bright with good visibility, and the sea was not too rough, but the wind was inclined to be squally. In a bare hour, the watchers reckoned, she would be dropping anchor in Spithead, and they saw the young men, in anticipation of a happy home-coming, crowding the rail to watch out for all the familiar landmarks.

Then, with appalling suddenness, a black cloud, driving before the strong breeze, hit the surface of the sea quite close to the ship, with a violent outburst of wind and a scurry of horizontal snow. One moment the watchers on shore saw the ship quite clearly: the next, she had entered the cloud and was lost to view. She never re-emerged. When the squall passed, the sea where she had been was completely empty. They rubbed their eyes in total disbelief. But it was true. Caught quite suddenly in that tremendous blast, the *Eurydice* had capsized and gone straight to the bottom. Of her total complement of officers and men, 200 in all, only six – all young seamen – were ever seen again. Every available boat was launched from the beach, and the six were picked up alive. But three of them were too far gone when the boats reached them, and they died from exhaustion and exposure before they could be landed. Even the three who did survive were too badly shaken to tell coherently what had happened. But it was clear enough. Hit by the sudden blast, the frigate had turned right over and failed to recover herself.

The disaster, happening so close to home, caused a great stir at the time, and all sorts of remedies were suggested in order to prevent such a tragedy from happening again. But they availed little, for in the very next year the *Atalanta,* a sister ship to the *Eurydice*, sailed from Portsmouth with another batch of young seamen, and – somehow and somewhere – disappeared without trace, carrying to his death, among others, the brilliant Lieutenant Philip Fisher, 'Jacky's' younger brother. From that day to this, nobody has any idea what happened to her.

Later on, they raised the *Eurydice* and brought her into Portsmouth. In the Victory Museum opposite the old flagship there stands to this day the training frigate's figurehead (Plate 10). And, still attached to it, there hangs a telescope. Probably, at the last moment somebody who had been inspecting the shore through his glass, clinging desperately to the figurehead, had sought un-availingly to relieve himself of the weight of it. It is a pathetic me-mento of a pathetic calamity – the only one of all our list in which the sheer violence of the sea has claimed its victim.

Last, it sounds odd to bring into a chapter entitled 'Accidents' the loss of two ships sunk by the enemy in the course of a full-scale war. Yet there seems no other place in which to mention them. The ships in question were armed trawlers, victims of air warfare in the Second World War. One was the *Cambrian,* which in 1940 hit a magnetic mine laid by aircraft. She was blown into two parts and sank on the edge of the shoal water south-east of the Horse Sand Fort. Next year, another trawler was hit while in the Swashway Channel, which runs south-west across the Spit Sand from the mouth of the harbour direct to the anchorage, and which is always much used by ships of fairly shallow draught. It speaks volumes for the aiming of the mine-laying Heinkel which laid its egg so unerringly plumb in the channel from the air and at night.

*Chapter V*

# THE EIGHTEENTH-CENTURY COURTS MARTIAL

A. *The Underlying Problem: Where The Navy Went Wrong*

During the eighteenth century three epoch-making courts martial shook the Royal Navy. All of them also in their day shook the quiet waters of Spithead, because they were held there or in Portsmouth Harbour. They must therefore have their place in this story. It is also necessary to try and understand what lay behind them: what in fact they meant to the Navy in terms of one of its most obvious functions – the winning of battles at sea.

That great body, already in most ways beginning to come into its own during the eighteenth century, unfortunately ran into troubled waters, both moral and technical, when it came to this very vital business of securing victory in sea-fights. From the early 1700s (in fact, from rather earlier) we were becoming more and more committed to a series of colonial wars with France, which lasted – with brief intervals – all through the century. Trade, empire and imperial dominion were at stake, and – quite frankly – we were by no means certain how to achieve our ends. Hitherto we had, on the whole, succeeded without undue difficulty in defeating our enemies at sea. But now we suddenly seemed to falter, and, from the moment when we defeated the French off Cape Barfleur in 1692 until we once more acquired the knack at the Battle of the Saints in 1782, a dreadful period of ninety years elapsed during which we failed entirely to impose our will upon our antagonists in pitched battles at sea.

The rot went deep. Among our sea-commanders there had developed two schools of thought – those who believed in taking the tactical offensive, and those who thought it wiser to act with some prudence: in other words, those who believed in attacking our enemies *à outrance*, and those who believed in avoiding defeat as a primary consideration. The protagonists of the first school were men like George Monk, Duke of Albemarle, and Prince Rupert – the products of our own Civil War and the subsequent maritime struggles with the Dutch Republic. The leader of the second school was James, Duke of York, the brother of Charles II and afterwards King James II. His guiding principle was adherence to rigid rules, which he hoped would curb the rashness of individual Captains, and allow the Commander-in-Chief to keep control over the whole action. After a struggle, it was the influence of James, Duke of York, which prevailed, thereby gradually wrapping up the Service in a cocoon-like attitude of mind – where pitched battles were concerned – which, while admittedly allowing the Commander-in-Chief to keep control of any action, also contrived to hamstring individual initiative. The Service was delivered over to the mercy of that set of hide-bound rules known as 'the Fighting Instructions'.

Now rules, as such, are good and necessary things in themselves. But obviously there are limits, and clearly something is radically wrong when a Commander who obeys the rules yet fails to win the battle is regarded as the hero of the day because he did not lose the battle nor break the rules, while the man who, using his initiative, contrived to lose his battle, was seriously punished for it. Sir George Rooke, the conqueror of Gibraltar, was here a particular sinner. His Permanent Fighting Instructions of 1704 drove the last nails into the coffin of initiative at sea.

To such a point had we come in 1744, when the War of Austrian Succession was upon us after a prolonged period – for those days – of relative peace. During that period the Fighting Instructions had reached an immensely dangerous predominance. The Admiralty's Official Instructions now meant everything, demanding absolute obedience from everybody. Break the Instructions, and, sure as Fate, an offending commanding officer would instantly be broken too!

12. Catherine of Braganza being greeted by James Duke of York on her arrival at Portsmouth, 1662. The Isle of Wight lies beyond the fleet in Spithead on the right

THE MANER OF THE QUEENES MA.^{ties}. LANDING AT PÓRTSMOUTH. DIS EMBARCASÃO DE RAINHA DA GRAN BRETÁN.EM PÓRTSMVTH ~5 mm

13. Spithead Review, 1773. George III on the *Barfleur* (left centre) is being saluted by the fleet

14. The *Lightning* steamer towing the *Royal Sovereign* (with the Duke of Clarence on board) into Portsmouth, 1827

B. *The Toulon Courts Martial*

Admiral Thomas Mathews was an old hand in command. He had been a Captain ever since the days of the War of the Spanish Succession, when he had been the colleague of men like George Rooke and Cloudisley Shovell. And now, in the new war which began in 1744, he was in command of our Mediterranean fleet. Senior as he was in rank, though, he was not a particularly great man – fussy, rather quarrelsome and all too prone to stand on his own dignity. Neither his equals nor his inferiors loved him. His own Admiralty did not trust him.

His plain duty in the Mediterranean was to attack the Spanish fleet, suspected at that moment of making common cause with the French Navy. And this he went out to do. But he was in charge of a far from competent fleet – its individual ships commanded by elderly and far from competent Captains – for peace, neither then nor at any other time, makes for even average efficiency.

It was even worse for him, though, because he sailed with all his battle-plans ready made for him – all written down in black and white not really by himself, but by the Admiralty. Those precious Instructions, official and Admiralty-inspired as they were, governed his every action. Among other things they laid down exactly how and when he should attack his enemy. At all costs he was to keep to windward of him, and on no account whatsoever was he to sail down to attack him until his own van was exactly aligned with the enemy's van, his own centre exactly opposite the enemy's centre and his rear exactly opposite his rear. The lines, in short, must be absolutely conterminous, with no overlappings anywhere. Only then could he allow himself to attack.

But observe the *woodenness* of it! No tactical advantage was to be taken on any account of circumstance. If by any chance the weather offered him any temporary advantage, he must deny himself the opportunity!

When he reached the French coast off their port of Toulon, he found that the Spanish squadron had joined with the French, and that the combined fleet of his enemies was sailing south, bent upon mischief either inside or outside the Straits of Gibraltar. Securing the wind, he conformed as best he could with their movements.

But the sea – even the Mediterranean Sea – is no mill-pond, and he soon found himself well behind station. His van, which should have been opposite the enemy's van, could only with difficulty reach a point opposite the enemy's centre, while his own centre could only reach the enemy's rear. Meanwhile, on a rising wind, his adversaries bid fair to escape him altogether.

Now Mathews was quite intelligent enough to realize that this would never do. Let them escape him now, and he might never come up with them again. So, after prolonged straining to get his division opposite the enemy's centre (and therefore in the only position in which his instructions would allow him to fight) as evening drew on, he came to his great decision. He turned his own flagship down-wind and directly towards the enemy ship which was at that moment opposite him. Make no mistake about it. Though this was the natural thing to do, it was for that day a distinctly heroic move.

But he was reckoning without the pernicious drag of those overpowerful Fighting Instructions. At once everything began to go wrong. A few of his immediate neighbours – his natural 'Seconds' – followed him in his turn. But none of the others did. Why? Because their Captains were as completely enslaved as he was to these absurd Instructions. Every man knew as well as Mathews did what those Instructions said, and everyone knew in his heart that to disobey them meant, under the circumstances, professional death to himself. So, generally inexperienced in ship-command as they were, and now caught in two minds, they did the worst possible thing, which was *nothing*. They did not follow their overbold leader down–wind towards the enemy. They just remained where they were.

To add to his troubles, Mathews's own Second-in-Command, responsible for his rear, seems deliberately to have gone sour on his superior. Meticulously (he afterwards said) he 'obeyed the Instructions' though this committed him to attack a piece of sea entirely innocent of all enemy shipping. Under such distressing circumstances, it is hardly necessary to say, the approach of the British fleet was a complete fiasco.

But in the sequel it was something a good deal worse than that.

The Admiralty – which, as all good men doubtless knew, was really to blame – took this opportunity to 'justify' itself by instituting a vast series of courts martial embracing all ranks of the Navy, but especially the Captains and the Flag Officers. Such a washing of dirty linen in public has never happened before or since in the Navy's long history. And by the time that all the trials were finished, *everyone* was proved guilty, if only of gross incapacity to hold command in His Majesty's Navy. And by the time that the breeze had settled again over Spithead and Portsmouth, the Navy's reputation lay in tatters.

By far the most important and damaging trial was that of Mathews himself, brought into court at the instance of his Second-in-Command – another veteran named Lestock (who was, incidentally, Mathews's arch-enemy). In June 1747, the Admiral was sentenced to be dismissed from the Service, and he was never forgiven, nor employed again. Public opinion settled upon Lestock as the villain of the piece, and he too was tried. But he left the court without a stain upon his character – because, forsooth, he had not broken the Fighting Instructions – and he was soon employed again. What the Court really had against the Admiral was never exactly specified. But Public Opinion held, with no uncertain voice, that he was really cashiered because he had dared to flout the Fighting Instructions. Herein lay the real tragedy of the affair. Here, men said – and said loudly – was an Admiral broken for displaying a spark of initiative! And thereafter, for the next thirty-eight years, the iniquitous Instructions held the field unchallenged. It was a fatal blow to all naval talent.

In just one direction, however, there was a silver lining to the louring cloud of frustration – just one way in which the incubus of the Instructions could be overcome. All that has been said so far has applied only to pitched battles with our foes: and so long as the enemy showed signs of standing up to us on the battlefield these soul-destroying orders held good. But, supposing that the enemy showed any signs of not standing up to us, but of running away and avoiding action – then the Fighting Instructions empowered our Admirals to take such steps as they thought fit to bring on a set action. Orders could be given in such circumstances for a *General*

*Chase.* If the enemy failed to set up a line of battle, the English Commander-in-Chief might at his discretion use his ships as he would without let or hindrance. He could even go in chase of the enemy and seek to demolish him at leisure. An order for General Chase absolved him from all responsibility in the matter. This too, was quite an absurd state of things, because it made any enterprising English Commander liable, when the moment came, to take the risk, and pursue that enemy with all the means at his disposal. And – during that bad patch of ninety years – the temptation imposed upon him of considering that the enemy was *not* standing became quite irresistible. Thus, during that long period the English fleet was not utterly debarred from victory; for, sometimes, the Commander-in-Chief who chose to regard the enemy as running away, might order General Chase and follow him – even if the said enemy was not in fact running away at all. Indeed, *all* the victories that we won during those ninety sterile years – and there were a few of them – were won by dispensing with the Line and by taking the risk of General Chase.

But a risk it was, and none but the really venturesome would be prepared to take it, because the penalty for failure was so very severe. Yet there were always a few really outstanding men who were so prepared, and to stand by the consequences when or if they failed. And sometimes they won battles. Of this sort was the action fought off Cape Passaro in 1719 by Admiral Sir George Byng, father of the unfortunate Admiral John Byng whose fate we shall recount shortly. He fell in with a weak Spanish fleet, renounced Fighting Instructions altogether, and ordered General Chase after the enemy from the start. He succeeded in winning quite a decisive victory, for which he earned all the credit which he so richly deserved. Three years after Toulon, also, and in this same War of the Austrian Succession, on no less than two occasions – both in the year 1747 – two outstandingly capable officers both secured smart and important victories by ignoring 'the Line' altogether. The first was George Lord Anson who in this way defeated the French fleet in the action known as 'First Finisterre'. Then, later in the same year, that bravest and most dashing of all our mid-eighteenth century naval Commanders, Sir Edward Hawke, then a junior

Rear-Admiral, had equal success in the second battle off Cape Finisterre. Moreover, in the next war – that of the 'Seven Years' – he repeated his performance in an even more striking manner in that classic action fought amid the shoals and tempests in Quiberon Bay in 1759. Edward Hawke was indeed our most enterprising and fearless officer during that dark period. For twice in his own lifetime he won decisive battles against not only our enemies but also against the absurdities of the Conterminous Line. Once too, during the War of American Independence, Admiral Sir George Rodney brought off a very successful 'Chase' action in the famous 'Moonlight Battle'.

To return for a moment to the unfortunate Mathews. He knew the futility of the Instructions, and he had the guts to rebel against that futility. Unfortunately for his reputation, however, he rebelled in the wrong way. The right way, in this ludicrous context, would have been to pretend that the enemy was running away (which, in this case, was very nearly true) and to follow him, dispensing with his formal line and flying the signal for General Chase. Instead, seeing the enemy, though retreating, to be in line of battle, he did not quite dare to go the whole hog and dispense with the formal line altogether. He chose rather to defy that part of the Instructions which insisted upon the Conterminous Line: and, as a breaker of this more-than-sacred order, he laid himself wide open to disaster, particularly as, for all his disobedience, he failed to win. So, though far from being either a talented or an amiable man, he does deserve our sympathy. At least he *tried* to win!

### c. *The Minorca Court Martial*

Yet such dashing men as Hawke and Rodney were still the exceptions and never the rule. Much more often we find English Commanders – not bad ones either – who remained hamstrung by the ineptitudes of the system, and who, though they strove gallantly enough to make bricks without straw, sometimes failed egregiously (and occasionally fatally to themselves) against the loaded odds.

The classic example of all time was the case of poor Admiral John Byng, who at the outbreak of the Seven Years' War – that war which, more than any other, was to win world dominion for us – was dispatched from England in 1756 with a most indifferently-equipped fleet, to relieve the island of Minorca, closely beset by the French.

The story is pitiful. It is an unredeemed tragedy. Like Mathews before him, Byng was neither a great Commander nor a great man. Still, he was a respectable, hardworking and conscientious soul, and for years he had held high and important commands in the Navy. If he had one weakness greater than others, perhaps it was that he took too sombre a view of things and was by nature something of a pessimist. Thus when he was appointed to the Mediterranean, all his friends assured him that the policy which sent him was a faulty one which could not possibly work out right: that the fleet they were giving him was too small and weak, too badly equipped to do what they were asking of him: in short, that the relief of Minorca at such a time and with such a force was a plain impossibility. And poor Byng believed them!

The trouble was that they were largely correct in their fears: and so was he. No one in England – or at any rate in the English Government – had any idea how to run a war. The Prime Minister – the Duke of Newcastle – though a prize string-puller, was a child on the subject. William Pitt the Elder, who had plenty of warlike ideas, was not allowed by King George II to hold any office at all. So in the event the French surprised us, and mounted a full-scale assault upon Minorca, hoping that we would panic, and send one or more of our leading officers – Anson, Hawke or Boscawen – scurrying out there. We resisted the temptation to do this, yet erred in taking the threat too lightly. We sent out a small, ill-found force and a rather small and defeatist Commander.

In apportioning the blame for the disaster which followed, one must not forget for an instant who it was who sent out the expedition in the first place – who, therefore, was *au fond* responsible for it. That, beyond any doubt at all, was the corrupt and inefficient government of the day. In no case can these men escape the blame; the fault was entirely theirs. They deliberately sent out too small a fleet under too small a Commander: and, not unnaturally, he failed. He failed badly, yet the Government which sent him, like all weak people, were too cowardly to consider taking the blame when things inevitably went wrong. The Prime Minister, the fussy, ineffectual Newcastle, was the main culprit. Yet the blame cannot be allowed to rest entirely on his unworthy shoulders. It must be shared by far better and abler men – William Pitt himself, Anson, the Head of the Navy, and, above all, Dettingen George, King of England. All, from the very start, were scandalously prejudiced against poor Byng, and pusillanimously intent upon shuffling off the blame when things began to go wrong. In fact – it is clear now – from start to finish the Admiral had no chance at all.

He sailed to Gibraltar with orders to pick up reinforcements from its rather spiritless Governor, a man almost as defeatist as Byng himself. This worthy refused all his requests point-blank, feeling, it seems, that any assistance he might give to the fleet could only weaken the defence of the Rock. So Byng, very tamely, did not insist upon having the marines to which he was entitled in his orders, but went on to Minorca without them, quite convinced, poor fellow, that his campaign was doomed to failure.

Once there, he found the French fleet, of much the same force as his own, barring his way to the island, having recently escorted a French army destined to capture, and occupy, the great harbour of Port Mahon. The enemy commander, the gallant but not particularly brilliant Marquis de la Galissonière, at least knew his business. He drew up his ships to the south of the island, covering the army which he clearly must defend. The action – a somewhat half-hearted affair – then took place. The Frenchmen certainly did not run, so that Byng (even if he had had it in him) could not legitimately consider that General Chase was permissible. Each Admiral now drew up his fleet in line ahead (though the lines were by no means parallel) according to the accepted notions of fighting. Yet within these limits de la Galissonière did refuse action – he allowed his ships to fall away to leeward. So now it was Byng's unenviable duty to fall upon him, while keeping his own line strictly conterminous with that of the enemy – a thing which was nigh impossible – and engage him as best he could. He tried, but could not manage it. Thus he found himself in approximately the same dilemma as had faced Mathews at Toulon twelve years before.

But now the British Admiral did show considerable tactical ability. He tried a manoeuvre known as 'approach by Lasking'.[1] Unfortunately, however, it was not a manoeuvre acknowledged by the Fighting Instructions which bound him, and there was no statutory signal for it. So – once more – he did not receive that support from his Captains to which he felt himself entitled. And he failed again. A scrappy, indecisive action ensued, in which neither fleet sustained really serious damage. But Byng had so far the best of it that Galissonière thought fit to break off the action and retreat to the north of Minorca.

So far, undoubtedly, the tactical advantage lay with Byng, who had at least driven his enemy from the field of battle, on which he passed the night. All he had to do, it would seem, was to hold his ground, and await the starvation of the French army landed on the island; for he was now in a position to prevent supplies arriving from France.

But Byng, the essential defeatist, unluckily did not see it quite like that. As always happened in Anglo-French contests, he could not fail to see that he was much more damaged aloft than the enemy was – for the French always fired on the upward roll of their ships so as to hit masts, yards and sails and so impair our mobility, while the English, firing on the downward roll, sent their roundshot into the Frenchmen's hulls, causing heavy casualties to personel, but no great loss of sail-power. In fact, compared with Galissonière's, Byng's fleet was now relatively immobile. A wave of pessimism therefore passed over him. What if Galissonière were to attack again, and cut his line of retreat? So he called a council of war – often the sign of a man who is uncertain of himself – seeking probably to share the responsibility with others. And that council – doubtless influenced by its leader's defeatism – recommended him to retire upon Gibraltar. This was tragic advice. Having gained a tactical success, he now allowed himself to make a strategic blunder of the first order. He left the field to the enemy, and sailed back to Gibraltar. It was a blunder, and a bad one, unworthy of a British Commander-in-Chief. For more than a month after his

---

[1] Lasking: sailing with ships in line on parallel courses, neither ahead nor abreast of one another, but somewhere between the two.

departure, the plucky English garrison at Port Mahon held out. Then it surrendered, and Minorca was lost.

The British public was not accustomed to failures of this kind; and on hearing the news, broadsheet writers, pamphleteers and cartoonists joined in one loud shout of vilification. Someone must pay for it, and that someone was obviously the Admiral. But the public was, as it almost always is, ill-informed. Moreover, this time, there were many people who must have known the truth. To us now, it seems only too clear that the trouble lay with sending out the wrong man; and someone should have had the pluck to say so. But no. At once the guilty perceived that they had a heaven-sent scapegoat to shelter behind, and pusillanimity in high places was all but universal. The Government itself knew well enough where the blame lay. But the Government had no intention whatever of saying so. 'Yes, yes,' quoth the Prime Minister to his cronies and his critics, 'we'll hang him, of course. Yes, yes.' And that, regrettable as it is to have to admit it, is precisely what the Government resolved to do: and did do – only, at the last, common decency allowed them to shoot him.

Calumny after calumny pursued the wretched man. He was accused of Jacobitism, of selling his country to the enemy, of rank cowardice in action. One facetious lampooner cried,

> I said unto brave West[1] 'Take the Van!
>   Take the Van!'
> I said unto brave West, 'Take the Van!'
> I said unto brave West, 'since you like fighting best,
>   I in the rear will rest.
> Take the Van!'

while a somewhat more polished vilifier wrote,

> We have lately been told
> Of two admirals bold
>   Who engaged in a terrible fight.
> They met after noon
> Which I think was too soon,
>   For they both ran away before night!

Twentieth-century propaganda has nothing on it!

[1] Byng's Second-in-Command, Temple West.

He was brought back to England under close arrest, though as
yet untried; and, once home, he was isolated on the top floor of
Queen Anne building at the Royal Hospital in Greenwich. Here
the Governor treated him with the utmost spite, sending in workmen to block up his window with stout bars of iron, lest he should
fling himself out and so cheat 'Justice' of her prey. But when, at the
end of December, a court was appointed to try him, he was
removed with ignominy to Portsmouth. The court martial, of
course, had to be a naval one, and four Admirals and nine Captains
met to try the case on board the *St George*. The President of the
court was a certain Admiral Thomas Smith, known to his con-
temporaries as 'Tom of Ten Thousand'. The charge was based
upon the Twelfth Paragraph of the Articles of War, the naval code
of discipline introduced some eighty years before by James, Duke
of York.

But thereby hangs a tale, most sinister for poor Byng. There was
in fact, no provision at all in the Articles of War for misdemeanours
committed anywhere else save on the battlefield itself. It was not
intended to deal with Admirals' conduct at any other time. But the
Articles had to be used because there were no others. Up till quite
recently the paragraph in question had read,

> Every person in the fleet who, through cowardice, negligence or
> disaffection, shall in time of action, withdraw, or not come into
> the fight or engagement, or shall not do his utmost to take or
> destroy every ship which it shall be his duty to engage; and to
> assist all and every of His Majesty's ships, or those of his allies,
> which it shall be his duty to assist and relieve; every such person
> so offending, and being convicted thereof by the sentence of a
> court martial, shall suffer death, *or such other punishment as the
> circumstances of the offense shall deserve, and the court martial
> shall judge fit.*

But, in the War of the Austrian Succession just ended,
certain miscarriages of justice, and the tendencies of over-lenient
courts martial to take too much upon themselves, had caused the
more merciful penalty to be ruled out. And now no alternative

but death remained. There can be little doubt why this had been done – the change had been made merely to reserve the prerogative of mercy to the Crown.

And – now – the Crown's prerogative was to be withheld – deliberately!

All Byng's judges were professional naval officers of high standing. There was never any intention on their part to act wrongly or deceitfully. For a whole month, with all formalities strictly preserved, that court sat, plying the accused, the witnesses for the prosecution and those for the defence with every relevant question. And at the end of that time the Court arrived at its decision and pronounced sentence: and decision and sentence were unanimous. He was acquitted of cowardice; he was acquitted of treachery. But they did not think it possible to acquit him of failure to do all that was feasible to bring to a happy conclusion the work with which he had been entrusted. So they convicted him of negligence, with the strongest possible recommendation to mercy. But – under the circumstances – that was meaningless. As the law then stood, the only punishment for negligence was death: and this sentence they had to pass upon him.

Europe – including the French but, of course, excluding his guilty compatriots – with one accord besought the King to execute his well-known prerogative of mercy. But the harsh old Hanoverian thought he knew better. To all pleas for mercy he made the same reply – 'Was the sentence of the court at fault?' Well, it was not – though criminally cruel, it was what the Law exacted. 'So,' said the King, 'it shall stand!'

And stand it did. One March morning in 1757, a party of marines, lined up upon the quarterdeck of the French prize *Monarque*, shot the Admiral at point-blank range (Plate 11). His demeanour, both then and throughout his long ordeal, impressed everyone who witnessed it. Surely 'nothing in his life became him like the leaving it.'

Yet, in equity, the whole thing had been a rather sordid farce from first to last. The court had, in effect, been trying him for the wrong thing. In the battle itself – save for the relative trivia imposed upon him by those asinine Instructions – he had scarcely put a foot wrong. Yet he had – and everyone knew it – been guilty of a serious – and disgraceful – dereliction of duty. He had failed, not so much tactically, as strategically and morally. He had sailed away, leaving his own compatriots in the lurch. And for that, morally, he deserved severe punishment. For that strategical error alone he should no doubt have paid with a blasted career. He should certainly never have been employed again.

But nothing worse. To shoot him for any such mistake was plain barbarity. They hadn't even tried him for it. For this error stemmed from the council room of his flagship: not from his own quarter-deck in battle. And not once, in all the thousands of questions asked or discussed at the court martial, did anyone ever raise the point of why he had withdrawn, or whether he should or should not have done so. To his judges such questions would have been *ultra vires*, and, of course, they knew it. In short, he was shot for a trivial tactical offence which he had barely committed; not for the serious strategical one for which they had not tried him.

Voltaire, who joined the effort to get Byng pardoned, put his finger on the weak spot in the English case. It is very well known what his *Candide* had to say about it:

En causant ainsi ils abordèrent à Portsmouth; une multitude de peuple couvrait le rivage, et regardait attentivement un assez gros homme qui était à genoux, les yeux bandés, sur le tillac d'un des vaisseaux de la flotte; quatre soldats, postés vis-à-vis de cet homme, lui tirèrent chacun trois balles dans le crâne le plus paisiblement du monde, et toute l'assemblée s'en retourna extrêmement satisfaite. 'Qu'est-ce donc que tout ceci?' dit Candide, 'et quel Démon exerce partout son empire?'. Il demanda qui était ce gros homme qu'on venait de tuer en cérémonie. 'C'est un Amiral', lui répondit-on. 'Et pourquoi tuer cet Amiral?' 'C'est', lui dit-on, 'parce qu'il n'a pas fait tuer assez de monde; il a livré un combat à un Amiral français, et on a trouvé qu'il n'était pas assez près de lui.' 'Mais', dit Candide, 'l'Amiral français était aussi loin de l'Amiral anglais que celui-ci l'était de l'autre!' 'Cela est incontestable', lui repliqua-t-on, 'mais dans ce pays-ci il est bon de tuer de temps en temps un Amiral pour encourager les autres'.[1]

It is cruel satire, but it contains an essential truth. The British public is the devil when crossed. 'Things have gone demonstrably wrong. Therefore someone needs trouncing. So let's trounce him and say no more about it!'

But Englishmen are never persistent haters. Let them but see one of their number downed, hounded and obviously being bullied, and they instantly relent. Long before the trial was over the public mood had completely changed. Once it had been, 'Hang the villain!': now it was, 'Poor old chap! Why are they all harrying him?' So, when the waters of Spithead on that blustery March day were furrowed by the endless keels of people who came out to look at the spectacle, what did they feel? For the original culprit, nothing but pure pity. Yet they still suspected depravity in high places – the cowardice of Newcastle, the harshness of the King in withholding his pardon. For instinctively, the English usually know that two wrongs don't make a right.

Rather less than three years later, Dettingen George departed this life. And, when his time came, was *his* judge more merciful to him than he had been to his Admiral? If we are Christians, we may be quite sure that he was!

---

[1] Talking thus they came ashore at Portsmouth. A crowd of people covered the shore line and closely watched a rather big man who was kneeling blindfolded on the poop of one of the ships of war. Four soldiers, standing facing him, each fired three shots into his skull in the most peaceful manner in the world, and the whole gathering went away deeply satisfied. 'Whatever is all this, then?' asked Candide. 'What demon is it that holds sway everywhere?' He asked them who the big man was who had been ceremoniously slain. 'It was an Admiral', he was told. 'And why kill this Admiral?' 'Because', he was told, 'he has not had enough people killed. He gave battle to a French Admiral, and they have decided that he did not get close enough to him.' 'But,' said Candide, 'the French Admiral was as far away from the English Admiral as the English one was from the French.' 'That is not to be denied,' they replied, 'but in this country it is a good thing to kill an Admiral now and then, to encourage the others.'

## D. *The Ushant Court Martial*

The third occasion during the eighteenth century in which the navy's dirty linen was publicly washed happened in 1778, at the outbreak of the next war against France. For three years before this the colonists of North America had been in rebellion against their mother country. Then our old enemy decided upon a war of revenge, to recover, if she could, the ground she had lost in the Seven Years' War. Since that war had ended, a regular renaissance had occurred in the French Navy. For once in a way the whole country had come forward to build up the fleet – for once in a way Frenchmen did not set their army first, but seemed to realize for a moment that, in any struggle with Great Britain, she must be strong at sea – stronger even than England. So, by 1778 she was ready, with a battle fleet of sixty well-found ships of the line, with dockyards and arsenals in a high degree of preparedness, and with a corps of officers new-trained, and – for the first time – better-trained than those of Great Britain.

At the same time, unfortunately for us, while French naval power was steadily on the rise, the British Navy was going through one of those periods of decline which punctuated the eighteenth century. Lord North, the principal 'King's Friend' and the King's Prime Minister, was firmly in the saddle at Westminster while, just up the road in Whitehall, John, Fourth Earl of Sandwich, was in charge at the Admiralty. Though personally dissolute, Sandwich was not perhaps so deep in political intrigue as his colleagues. But everywhere else crass favouritism was rife. Practically all offices of state were already held by King's Friends, while all the old evils of naval and dockyard maladministration had reappeared. Corruption in high places was universal: speculation everywhere was all-pervading. In 1763, when all over the world victory was our portion, the Royal Navy had been, by a very wide margin, the strongest on earth. By 1778 it was very doubtful whether it was as strong as that of France alone.

There was nothing wrong – in theory – with the leading officers in our Service. Hawke was still alive, though too old to command afloat. There remained also Richard Howe, George Rodney, Augustus Keppel and Samuel Barrington. Howe was sent out to

New York, where we had already been fighting the colonists for three years. Rodney, already an oldish man, had during the years of peace gone to live in France, where unfortunately he had fallen into debt so that he could not leave the country.

The next man on the list was Keppel, already an Admiral of the Blue and, like all too many of our senior officers at that time, a Member of Parliament. Here he was rather exceptional, because he was not a King's Friend, but just an old-fashioned patriot who held that politics should be kept out of the Navy altogether. When he was approached by Sandwich and invited to take on the Channel fleet, he had hesitated. He had no use for the King's Friends; he was not sure of Lord Sandwich. But the First Lord used all his wiles to catch him, promising that the Channel fleet was in a perfect state of readiness: that no less than forty-two ships of the line were in commission, with thirty-five of them all manned, victualled and quite ready for sea. Rather unwillingly, Keppel allowed himself to be persuaded, and accepted the command. But, on hurrying down to Portsmouth to see what was ready and what was not, he discovered to his horror that only twenty were in commission at all, and that not more than six of these were 'fit to meet a seaman's eye'. Tradition says that, in merry vein, he poked playfully at the main mast of one of the 'ready' ships with his cane, which sank into the rotten wood and disappeared from sight. But he went to work with a will, and the Admiralty, momentarily contrite, seemed willing enough to help him.

As soon as possible – but really much too late, because naval efficiency is never a thing that can be hurried – he contrived to get twenty sail ready for service, with sufficient crews to work them. With these he sailed about the middle of June. But the Admiralty, fearing his reputation as a determined fighter, then ordered him quite definitely to return to Portsmouth if he found himself outnumbered. He went cruising off Ushant, where he came upon not less than thirty-two French sail all ready for action. So, unwillingly, he obeyed orders, and returned to Spithead.

Now Keppel was not, perhaps, among the very top flight of British naval commanders, but he was a good deal better than the pessimist Byng, and far above the cantankerous Mathews. At the lowest he was a man of resolution, a highly efficient officer, and deservedly very popular both with his officers and his men: and there was no reason why, if given proper support from above, he should not have done well enough. When he set out again, with thirty ships, he determined that, this time, he would engage the enemy. With characteristic prudence, however, the French Admiral – d'Orvilliers – avoided him, and sailed straight out into the Atlantic. Keppel followed him, and chased him out into the Western Ocean for four full days, during which he gradually gained upon the enemy, though in doing so his own line fell into considerable disorder. Then d'Orvilliers, seeing that he would soon be caught, suddenly turned upon the English, wore his fleet (i.e. went about by turning down-wind) and came down upon Keppel from the windward, seeking to engage him on opposite tacks, so that the fleets would pass each other and then draw clear.

The battle which followed, fought many miles out from land in the Atlantic, has always been known, for lack of a better name, as the Battle of Ushant, though actually that island lies a long way to the east. The English fleet, though in considerable disarray, still had one considerable advantage. Owing to the weather, and the big Atlantic swell, the enemy found themselves unable to open their lower gun-ports, and so to fire their heaviest artillery. However, in the first phase of the action the fleets passed each other at fairly close range, the English (as usual) doing considerable execution on the hulls of the French ships, 'making the splinters fly', killing and wounding many of the enemy's men: while the French (also as usual) firing high, contrived to damage, in some ships seriously, the English masts and yards, without, however, inflicting too many casualties on their crews. When the fleets had drawn past each other, the British Second-in-Command leading the van – Sir Robert Harland, a most competent officer – tacked (i.e. turned into the wind) with a view to continuing the action by following the enemy on the *same* tack. But Keppel recalled him at once, and probably rightly because the whole fleet had suffered very unequally in the first encounter. Harland in the van had been engaged only for a short time, and only with the French rear, whereas Keppel himself had engaged both the enemy's centre and his rear. But the

English rear, commanded by the Third-in-Command, Sir Hugh Palliser, having sustained the fire of the whole French fleet, was so knocked about aloft that it could only with the utmost difficulty come round at all.

D'Orvilliers, having drawn clear, now looked back over his shoulder and saw a group of the worst-damaged of the British ships drifting to leeward of our line. He now saw his chance, if he would return, to attack, and even capture them. So he wore his fleet and came south again. But Keppel was in the position to guard against the threat. Seeing that Palliser and the rear squadron were well to the leeward of his own line, he himself deliberately sailed downwind, putting out at the same time the signal for 'line ahead'. There was really no chance of anyone in his senses misunderstanding that order. It was the only way in which the British fleet could get into line ahead again, and so obey those futile Fighting Instructions, which ordered it to be both 'in line ahead' and 'Conterminous with the enemy'. And so, of course, Harland in the van understood it, and hastened to conform.

Not so Palliser, however. Admittedly some of his ships were seriously knocked about aloft, but, after all, he was only being asked to fall down-wind into his proper place behind the British centre. On seeing the signal, he acknowledged it (which showed that he had seen it). But he did nothing else. He did not even plead that his hurts prevented obedience. Keppel, mystified, repeated the signal, then repeated it again; but with no result. Fortunately Harland, having reached his station ahead of the centre, was now covering the lame English ships, so that they were safe enough. But, if the action was to be renewed that day, speed was clearly of the essence. So, in the end, Keppel took the extreme step of summoning all Palliser's ships individually by name to his own flag; and then at last they moved down-wind into their correct positions astern of him. But it was already too late, and before the whole line could be reformed, darkness had fallen on the ocean. And when the next day dawned, d'Orvilliers, who evidently feared a second round, had vanished.

Now Keppel, though he knew well enough that he had been ill-used by his Third-in-Command, was by nature a good-tempered man. He had no wish to repeat the kind of slanging-match which had occurred after the Battle of Toulon. In his despatch to the Admiralty, therefore, he reported that 'the spirited conduct of Sir Robert Harland, *Sir Hugh Palliser*, and the Captains of the fleet deserves much commendation.' It cannot have been quite true, but he doubtless hoped that by such generalizations he would keep all dirty-linen-washing out of the public eye. But it was really very forbearing of him, because he knew as well as anyone what a decisive victory over the enemy so early in the war would have been worth to Great Britain. We would have been spared the next four years of desperate struggle against defeat – especially when Spain, and later Holland, joined with France to humble us.

For all his forbearance, however, he was unsuccessful in keeping the peace. The villain of the affair was Sir Hugh Palliser, not only in failing to support his chief on the battlefield itself, but also – and even more so – in his later conduct. He was a staunch King's Friend who had recently held high posts in the Admiralty, whereas Keppel was, we recall, not really a politician – to whom, in the eyes of Lord North and his gang, no kudos should be allowed at all. Gradually the true story of what had happened seeped out into the newspapers. This was not at all to Palliser's credit, and he was furious. Like Keppel, he was a member of the House of Commons, and before anyone could stop him he was accusing his own Admiral of all sorts of misdemeanours across the floor of that august chamber. Keppel naturally defended himself, though he was very careful to add no fuel to the flame of Palliser's wrath. That worthy, however, was not to be appeased, and had no difficulty in inducing his political bosses to proceed against the Admiral, and to try him for his life before a court martial for 'misconduct and neglect of duty'. And this they did, convening a court of five Admirals and eight Captains on board the *Britannia* in Spithead in January 1779.

On paper it looked rather like a repetition of Byng's court martial of the last war, or perhaps even more like that of Mathews in the war before that. But actually things were very different now. All that was decent in the country was, from the start, on Keppel's side. North and the King's Friends were in a hopeless minority when it came to numbers. Although the Earl of Sandwich was not unpopular, Service public opinion among officers and on the lower deck was largely pro-Keppel. (Just think of the number of inns in the land called 'The Keppel's Head'. Pub-names are always a good measure of a man's contemporary popularity.) So the proceedings of the court, far from disgracing the Admiral, were one long triumph for him.

Palliser and his friends (the *King's* Friends) tried desperately hard to fasten the blame on the Admiral, descending even to the most questionable tactics. Thus it was discovered during the trial that the log of the Vice-flagship covering the most vital moments of the action had been tampered with – certain pages had been cut out and removed. This, of course, could only be helpful to Keppel, as were even some of the prosecution's witnesses. One, on being asked, 'Did Keppel run away?' hesitated a moment and then replied, rather grudgingly, 'If he ran away, I followed him!' 'And did *you* run away?' This was too much for the witness who, losing his temper, bellowed out, 'By God, I did not!'

Throughout, Keppel conducted his own defence, quietly and soberly, and long before the proceedings were over, the verdict of the court was certain. His friends had arranged for a signal-gun to be fired which would inform the anxious fleet in the Anchorage of the result. At last it came – 'The charges are ill-founded and malicious' were the words of the president, Admiral Smith. The guard-ship signalled the verdict to the fleet and every ship replied with a thunderous salute. The cheers from town and countryside were echoed all the way up the Portsmouth Road to London as a coach carried the news to town.

Now, of course, Palliser had to be tried for the sake of his own reputation. He was acquitted, partly because he was a King's Friend, partly because neither Keppel nor *his* friends worked very hard to get him punished. He was acquitted; but a rider was added to the verdict which said that, if his ship had been incapable of performing further manoeuvres, he should have informed the Admiral of the fact. It was, men said, such a 'censurious acquittal' as to be tantamount to a conviction.

In town, however, Palliser did not escape nearly so lightly, because a highly pro-Keppel mob attacked his London residence, entered it and smashed everything inside it to pieces.

Once more all over the country the lampooners and the penny-poets got to work. But, this time, they poured out their venom on Palliser, not Keppel: on the underling, not on the Admiral:

> (to be sung to the tune of '*God save the King*')
> Go, go thou base Sir Hugh,
> Vice-Admiral of the blue,
> Prithee be still!
> Ah what a wicked dog
> To splice the very log!
> Give him instead of grog
> A leaden pill!

Everyone now said that Keppel should take up the command of the fleet again, and without delay. But the Admiral himself had had enough of it, and he steadfastly refused to serve again so long as the King's Friends remained in power. We ought not to blame him over-much: it can have been no fun at all to place one's professional honour in such hands. And, in the following year, both Richard Howe and Samuel Barrington did the same thing. They too refused to hoist their flags again until the offence was removed.

This, however, was most serious for Great Britain. It meant that in 1779 and 1780 – when all Europe was combining against us – we had nothing but second-line Admirals to call upon to defend us. And so the crisis went on until, in 1781 and still more in 1782, George Rodney came to England's rescue. Although employed by the King's Friends, he contrived to win for us the crushing victory of the Saints in April 1782. This was the battle – the first stand-up victory for ninety years – which instantly put paid to all the nonsense and bad blood caused by the Fighting Instructions. These curiosities survived all right – after all, one must have rules – but they were now relegated to their proper place, as *Admiral's* Instructions and no longer *Official* Instructions.

Incidentally, it is rather ironical to recall that the vital battle had hardly been won when Rodney's relief (who was not a King's Friend) arrived and superseded him. For North and Company had at last fallen from power, and, with them, King George's pretensions to 'be a King' in his own right had gone for ever.

After this, it need hardly be said, there were courts martial a-plenty at Spithead and elsewhere. But they never again so blatantly exposed Britain's weaknesses to the gaze of a hostile world. And never again was a Commander-in-Chief to be brought to trial by his Second- or Third-in-Command. Obviously, that is not the best way to preserve fleet discipline or morale. Those joyous salvoes, ringing out over a happy Spithead, marked the end of an intolerable state of affairs. And once more an era of British victory at sea, unsurpassed in the navy's annals, put her far ahead of her rivals.

## Chapter VI

# MUTINY

Courts martial upon Admirals now became very rare indeed: but not other courts martial. There still existed that other offence which also involved legal action and punishment – Mutiny.

The most important, or at least the best-known, single event in all the long history of Spithead is probably the mutiny of the Channel Fleet lying there in the spring of 1797. But it was not the first occasion when this particular menace shook the morale of the fleets which habitually anchored there. The refusal of the seamen of Britain to do their duty is always, *au fond,* a question of pure economics. At the outbreak of the great Civil War in 1642, the men had preferred the terms offered them by Parliament to those offered by the King: and they were doubtless technically guilty of the crime of mutiny. But we shall not consider it as mutiny here, but rather as Constitutional Rebellion, because on that occasion everyone in the Fleet, officers and men alike, had refused to serve any longer and had gone over to the other side. And their decision, it can be argued, made all the difference in settling the issue of that war.

Again in 1688 there was disaffection in the fleet at Spithead. Once more the motive was an economic one, with a political tinge as well; and once more the leaders were the officers. In the autumn of that year the fleet had been mobilized to meet the threat of the Prince of Orange, who proposed to put his wife Mary (and perhaps himself) on the throne of England, displacing his un-popular Roman Catholic uncle and father in-law, James II. He had for good measure been invited to come over by the whole of the English Whig Party, and he had the Dutch Navy behind him. James's great naval adviser, Samuel Pepys, had been responsible for the mobilization, which, as one might expect, had proceeded without a hitch. But Pepys was not responsible for finding the money to pay for the fleet; and, with the Government on the point of crumbling away, no one had found the money, with the inevitable result that there was practically nothing left in the Treasury with which to pay and feed the men.

In October of that year the position was this: such ships and such Captains (less than half the whole) as still remained faithful to James lay at the Gunfleet, south of Harwich, under the command of Lord Dartmouth – almost the only Protestant leader remaining on James's side. He was charged with protecting London from invasion and with intercepting William of Orange, the larger half of the English fleet, and the Dutch Navy. But Dartmouth's fleet did not, as strategy demanded, try to prevent William from leaving his Dutch ports. It was hardly strong enough, or certain enough of itself, to attempt that. So the Prince was allowed to start and, after an abortive thrust at the East coast, turned about, and availing himself of what at the time was known as 'the Protestant Wind', ran west down the Channel and, coming at length to Torbay in Devon, landed at Brixham on November 5.

Meanwhile Dartmouth found himself bottled up at Gunfleet by that same easterly wind; and when at length he got out, he dithered about in the Channel and was far too late to prevent the Prince from landing. Then, the wind again favouring the invader by settling in the west, he had to put about once more and half-heartedly take refuge in Spithead. During all the rest of the crucial month of November, while the Prince was securing the whole of England, the fleet lay there at its moorings, doing nothing: not even trying to cut William's communications with Holland. No doubt adverse winds were in part responsible for Dartmouth's ineffectiveness. But the real cause lay with his Captains. Ever since their vigil at Gunfleet began, disaffection had been growing, until at Spithead it was widespread enough to immobilize the fleet. Most of the officers were by now, at best, lukewarm towards

James's cause; many had decided not to fight; and some had positively defected, like Captain George Churchill who went over to William pretending that his ship had sprung a leak. At the same time, 'the Captains . . . infused strange notions in the seamen', who were already querulous for their pay and better food. Dartmouth could do nothing to remedy all this. He was paralysed by want of hard cash and by the attitude of his officers. Indeed, he even refused, under compulsion, to allow James's son, the infant Prince of Wales, to escape from Portsmouth to the safety of France. But the agony did not last long. Within a month James himself had fled and Dartmouth had handed over his fleet to William's 'gracious protection'.

In the light of future events it was perhaps as well that the fleet was immobile during this time. If it had come out and attacked William's ships wherever it found them, there would inevitably have been bloodshed; which in its turn would have spoilt the proud boast of the Whigs that their glorious Revolution of 1688–9 was also the Bloodless Revolution. So this seems to be one of those rare occasions when mutiny positively paid a dividend; because a fleet at such odds with itself, we may be very sure, could never have reversed the verdict of the English Revolution. And, oddly enough, the next mutiny which comes up for discussion is undoubtedly another which paid a dividend, rather different, but even bigger.

The whole lay-out was, however, very different in 1797. This time the seamen refused with complete unanimity to obey their officers, thereby committing the undoubted crime of mutiny. And it was a particularly serious moment at which to commit it, because just then Great Britain was in the throes of a very great war – that against Revolutionary France. And this time again the outbreak was purely economic, though the economic causes underlying it were not the same as those which had obtained in 1688: at least, not exactly the same. For, then, the Government had ceased to pay wages at all, but, now, they *were* paying them, but not paying enough, and also – short-sightedly – they were allowing what they did pay to find its way all too often into the wrong pockets. And the reason why this so-called 'Breeze at Spithead' in 1797 was of such vital importance – economic importance – was that, clean contrary to almost every other known mutiny, it was virtually one-hundred-per-cent successful. Thus the mutineers were able to do what mutineers can so seldom do – impose their will upon their masters, and force their Government to give them a fair deal at last. Here for all time is the Seaman's Charter. Never again were they to be so grossly imposed upon.

The men had many grievances, but the main one – the one which they mentioned first – was still Pay. They said they did not get enough of it: and they claimed (and claimed rightly) that they did not receive nearly all of what *was* given. There was, first, the actual amount of wage. Despite the notorious rise in the cost of living – which, though irregular, was always going on – the rate of their wage had not risen since the time of Cromwell and the Commonwealth Government. Those sagacious men had raised the remuneration of the Ordinary Seaman to nineteen shillings a month, and the Able Seaman's to twenty-two and six, which in the 1650s was adequate, and perhaps even rather handsome. But it had long since ceased to be either. And another thing which undoubtedly shook the *amour propre* of the sailors was the fact that, some years before, the Government had actually increased the wages of its land forces to reach that well-known figure of 'a shilling a day'. This unquestionably wounded the poor seaman in a tender spot because – quite rightly – he regarded himself as constituting the first line of England's defence. And now the Soldier, even the common private, was drawing his twenty-eight shillings per lunar month where the Ordinary Seaman – the corresponding grade – was still receiving only nineteen shillings.

But this was not all, nor even probably the worst of it. All sorts of hazards stood between the wretched sailor and his miserable nineteen bob before he could touch it – anomalies which, though hardly mentioned at all by the seamen's leaders in 1797, would, to modern eyes, create monstrous grievances. For instance, it had long been the established custom not to pay wages at all until they were six months overdue; and for ships long in commission they were often much more overdue than that – even years behindhand. Not until a commission was over and the ship paid off could the seamen step ashore: nor was there any efficient provision for transferring any portion of what was owing to them to their dependents, though after 1758 – in theory – a minute fraction could be so paid. Further, even when at length a seaman left his ship, he received only a 'ticket', not the wages in cash. The actual money could sometimes be obtained only by a personal visit to the Pay Office on Tower Hill, and not always even there. And Tower Hill was a far step in those days from Chatham or Portsmouth, let alone Plymouth. The result was inevitable – an extensive traffic in pay-tickets, often at scandalous rates of discount, between the seamen and more or less professional ticket-buyers, who in their turn were in league, or sharing spoils, with all sorts of other interested parties, including the slop-sellers, sometimes (it is to be feared) the Pursers, and often 'ye gentlemen behind ye curtaine' – sinister name for the clerks of the Pay Office itself. Sometimes, too, when a man was transferred direct from one ship-commission to another, he never saw the wages owing to him from his first ship: and even if he received the ticket for them, he could not possibly cash it except through one of the buying fraternity, who would be sure to exact from him a commission of twenty or thirty per cent. It was all, in fact, a concerted swindle, highly developed and already hoary with age: but whoever might profit, there was never any doubt as to who lost – the seaman.

There was also – it sounds scarcely credible, but it is the strict truth – a special 'service' scale of weights and measures. In this scale the pound contained not 16 ounces but only 14, the odd two being retained as the 'perks' of the ship authority who purveyed the provisions – the Purser. Nor was this what the men were accustomed to call 'a Pusser's Trick'. This was the Law of the Land, and the two-ounce rake-off was actually a considerable part of the Purser's official salary. He had many other notorious tricks, too, which *were* illegal: but this was not one of them, and the seamen did not mention it in their first demand, though they added it, as we shall see, to the second.

The Spithead Mutiny lasted for almost exactly a month – from April 16 to May 15: and though in law it was one-hundred-per-cent mutiny, it was yet, paradoxically enough, a triumph of studious

moderation and common sense in all the seamen, leaders and
led alike. And though it seemed to place the country in a position
of appalling danger, yet even that danger was deliberately mini-
mized from the beginning by the seamen themselves, who at once
made it perfectly plain that, were the French fleet to put to sea
while they were 'out', they would instantly place the nation's
interests before their own, and be led out to fight by their own
(reinstated) officers. Mutiny no doubt should never be condoned
in any Service, but it is impossible not to feel, having regard both
the men's moderation and to the enormity of their grievances,
that this one was more excusable than any other before or since.

It is usually said that this 'Breeze' took the authorities completely
by surprise, though there is no reason why it should have done,
seeing that several British officers had informed the Admiralty
months before that something of the sort was in the wind. The
First Lord of the day, Lord Spencer, though not a naval officer,
was a thoroughly honest, honourable and able man. But he took
no heed of the warnings because, both to him and his fellow
Admiralty Lords, such a trouble from such a source seemed
frankly impossible. They knew of course that service in the Navy
was most unpopular; and they knew it for the best possible reasons
– that they always found the utmost difficulty in wartime in getting
men voluntarily to enlist. But this had always been so, and, save
for the fact that in this particular war (which was on a bigger scale
than any before it) the difficulties of recruitment had also been
greater than ever before, they could see no radical change in the
situation. Hitherto (though with difficulty) they always *had* secured
the men they wanted, either voluntarily or by force, and they supposed that things would be the same now, and that they would go
on being the same for ever. The men, they knew, were grumbling
over the shocking conditions under which they were compelled
to live. But they always had grumbled – there was nothing new
about that. And Authority's standard argument was something
like this: 'Needs must when the Devil drives! We have got, for
Britain's security, to have many thousands of sailors, and the
nation, at heart, is sensible enough to know it. We take all who
volunteer most willingly, and we make up the rest – since not

nearly enough ever do volunteer – by our system of sending out press-gangs to force our merchant seamen to serve in the Royal Ships during the time that war lasts.' This was of course Conscription, and that they realized, though they probably failed to see what a very unfair form of conscription it was. For it did not – as modern National Service does – take all the young men of the country, but only the seafaring part of the community.

Yet, even by the 1790s, the Government had been compelled to realize that the old-fashioned though simple methods of recruitment were becoming inadequate for the nation's needs: that the time had come, in fact, when, to raise sufficient numbers, they must go outside the sea-going profession and bring in a proportion of non-seagoers too. This is what the Prime Minister, William Pitt the Younger, had done in 1795 and 1796, when he had introduced his celebrated Quota Acts, which sought to supplement the volunteers and the pressed men with a certain percentage of others drawn from other walks of life. To this end the whole country, both towns and counties alike, had been told to provide a quota of men to serve in the fleet.[1] And these 'Quota-men', though still small in numbers, we shall find playing an altogether disproportionate part in the mutiny.

Why should this be so? The thing is almost psychological. The seaman population was a largely inbred society, composed almost exclusively of hereditary sailors. 'Once a seaman, always a seaman' was certainly the norm, and the profession had for so many centuries been brought up, as it were, in its own water-tight compartment, differing in a great many respects from members of other professions and even looking down on them. They were a hardy, almost uncouth, breed compared with other classes: entirely uneducated; when on their own element – the sea – quite remarkably efficient, ready-handed and ingenious; but, taken away from it, the merest children who, on shore, were well known for doing the silliest things. And, until very few years before, the seamen of Britain, as a class, had scarcely changed at all through the centuries. Right up to the time when men from other pro-

[1] E.g. Yorkshire, 1,081, Rutland, 23; London had to provide 5,704, Newcastle, 1,240 and Bristol, 666.

fessions began to join them, they were really incapable of looking after themselves anywhere else but on shipboard. And among other things that they were incapable of, they had no idea whatever of combining: which, in the competitive world that was fast emerging, was already becoming a prime necessity of life. They certainly were a down-trodden company, but they had no idea of how to improve their lot.

Now it is never – fortunately for *homo sapiens* – the brute beast, the cow or the sheep, that rebels. Nor was it the old seamen-class who, of their own initiative, mutinied. It was only when there came among them a new and, from the point of view of mere civilization, a superior breed – people who already knew a little more about what was what – that the seamen found instructors who could make them aware of their wrongs, and encourage them to improve their own conditions. And here were the necessary men – the teachers and leaders who taught and led them – the Quota-men.

They were not necessarily good teachers, or good leaders. At the Nore, where in the same year another and even more dangerous mutiny took place, they were on the whole bad teachers, bad leaders. But at Spithead, the Navy was much more fortunate. For, here, the leaders were great men: indeed surprisingly great men who conducted the whole outbreak with masterly *savoir faire* and real diplomatic skill. Those leaders indeed were among the wonders of their age, and they richly deserved all the success which stemmed from their leadership. We can now see, in fact, that they were not mere leaders of mutineers but something much more, and much more modern. They had most of the attributes of the modern strike-leader; and their leadership really turned the wholy mutiny into something much more like a modern strike – which, when all is said, is much more likely to succeed than was an old-time mutiny.

Up till 1797, though the whole of the Royal Navy had not done quite so well as the Nation expected, it was still universally re-garded as 'Britain's sheet anchor'. There was a confidence in it which was quite touching. 'Britannia, Rule the Waves', men sang: 'the Navy is invincible', they thought: 'the gallant British Tar is the Bulwark of the Country', they boasted. Everything else might go wrong: the Army might botch things, but not the Navy, which was brilliantly led, superbly efficient. Boney might threaten invasion, but while our ships stood between him and us, we could all sleep soundly in our beds.

Judge then the shock, the near-panic, when, with appalling suddenness, the country learned, on April 16, 1797, that the whole Channel Fleet had refused point-blank to raise its anchors when ordered to do so by its Admiral, Lord Bridport. At once the bottom fell out of the Englishmen's world. The *Navy* in open mutiny? It was fantastic, absurd! If that had happened, *anything* might happen – indeed, very soon *would* happen. As one of his Board told Lord Spencer, 'the event forms the most awful crisis that these kingdoms ever saw', and he was not exaggerating. At first, in fact, everyone was in despair – the politicians, the merchants, the bankers, the country gentry, the whole populace. It was all, wrote the *Annual Register,* so exceedingly unnatural, and even supposed to be so remote from possibility, that it is difficult to say whether surprise, grief or terror was the predominant feeling which it excited.

Now the public might well be astonished, but My Lords of the Admiralty had no grounds at all for surprise. Two whole years before, Admiral Philip Patton had submitted to Lord Spencer a long report, which proved beyond doubt that a general mutiny was possible at any time. It also stated with admirable directness the unpleasant fact that the rate of seaman-desertion was so great as to threaten the very existence of the Royal Navy. These phenomena – desertion and mutiny – are evidently closely connected: the second is often the sequel to the first. Individuals – if their lives are made wretched enough – will desert even though the penalty of death is exacted in the event of recapture: and desertion will go on so long as there is no thought of combined action on board. But once there is – once the men have sensed the possibility of combination – desertion may well (and probably will) be followed by open mutiny. After all, the penalty for the one is neither better nor worse than the penalty for the other – it is death in either case. So probably, once the feasibility of combination is realized, combined mutiny is on the whole preferable to individual desertion: and it has a better chance of succeeding.

This was happening now – had been happening in individual cases these many years. The *Bounty* mutiny of 1789 is only one example, where the crew of that vessel had risen against the tyranny of their officers in the Pacific. The men had prevailed for the time being, jettisoning their Commanding Officer, 'Bread-fruit' Bligh, in an open boat in mid-ocean. They fondly imagined that he could not survive: but by great pluck and fortitude he managed, after an epoch-making trip, to reach home safely. And, thereafter, the culprits were hunted like rats across the Seven Seas and, when taken, ruthlessly executed. There had been other mutinies: in Howe's fleet (in the *Culloden*) in 1794, and yet another in the same year in the *Windsor Castle* in the Mediterranean. Both were very ruthlessly suppressed – rather treacherously in the case of the *Culloden*. But all three were regarded by the authorities as exceptional, and doubtless they were, being caused either by the exceptional and excessive brutality of the officers in the ships concerned or else – and this is particularly true in the case of the *Bounty* – by the presence on board of someone capable of organizing mutiny: which in itself was an exceptional circumstance before the appearance of the Quota-men. (The ringleader in the *Bounty* was the well-educated and 'gentlemanly' Fletcher Christian, a Master's Mate – the highest rank then existing below a commissioned officer – who was promoted by Bligh himself earlier in the voyage to an acting-lieutenancy. He was never caught, but founded on Pitcairn Island the community which occupies it to this day.)

The case of the *Bounty* is typical of all mutinies. They happen when the men can find a leader better educated than themselves.

There was another thing, too, which the Admiralty knew all about. Petitions from disgruntled seamen were very far from uncommon. Its records contain literally hundreds of them, many quite touching in their faith in the fatherly nature of their Lordships. But to that august body – even to the usually imaginative Spencer – such documents were not meant to be attended to. They

127

were regarded simply as so many safety-valves, wherewith the 'tooth-sucking' sailor could let off steam. This is a fact, though it is very difficult to believe it after reading in bulk the vast numbers of these pathetic requests. Here are a few specimens.

(1) The Lieutenant (of the *Weazle* Sloop) often came on board drunk and amused himself 'by making us strip and ceasing [seizing] us up to the riggin and beating us with the end o'rope till we almost expire'.

(2) 'The ill-usage we have on board this ship forced us to fly to your Lordships the same as a child to its father. It is almost impossible for us to put it down in paper as cruel as it really is with flogging and abusing above humanity' (from the *Nassau*, 1795).

(3) 'The ill-treatment which we have and do receve from the tiriant of a Captain [Fraser; in the letter spelt Fraizere] from time to time, which is more than the spirits and harts of true English Man can cleaverly bear, for we are born free, but now we are slaves' (from the *Shannon*, 1796).

(4) 'Draft us on board any of His Majesty's ships. As we don't want to go to sea in the *Winchelsea* . . . our usage was more like Turks than of British seamen . . . we are nockt about so that we do not no what to do. Every man in her would sooner be sot [shot] at like a taregaite by muskettree than remain any longer in her' (from the *Winchelsea* at Spithead, 1793).

Of course Their Lordships knew very well that such brutal scenes were quite commonplace. Their only trouble was that they could not bring themselves to listen. But surely they should have had the sense to realize that all the hundreds of such plaints, all to the same tune, could not possibly be the lucubrations of mere tooth-suckers. It was a shocking lapse in their imagination!

In 1796 Spencer received another kind of letter, this time from the gallant Captain Thomas Pakenham. It was so reasonable and so out-spoken that it seems almost impossible that he could have ignored it. It is not about brutalities at all. It is simply about pay, and the unfairness of raising not only the soldiers' wages but also those of all ranks of naval officer without doing anything for the

15. Spithead Review, 1856. The Royal Yacht *Victoria and Albert II* is in the centre

16. Spithead Review, 1897. The pioneer *Turbinia* dashes through the fleet at over 30 knots

17. Spithead Review, 1953. In the foreground, left to right, Trinity House yacht *Patricia*, H.M.S. *Surprise* (acting as Royal Yacht), and H.M.S. *Redpole*

seamen. Surely, one would have thought, he must know that even
the lowliest worm must turn when trodden upon heavily enough
and long enough? But no. He acknowledged Pakenham's letter,
sincerely thanking him for putting him wise on such an important
question. Then he did nothing – nothing at all! After all, he was
a good and honest party politician, with all the politician's horror
of hearing the scandalized exclamations of his colleague, the
Chancellor of the Exchequer, inevitably evoked by a demand for a
general rise in pay for over 100,000 men. In his reply to Pakenham
there is such a wealth of time-serving blather as is scarcely credible.
It is Civil Service jargon to the power of x. What he actually
wrote was,

> Though undoubtedly [the matter is] one which we cannot
> but wish for a proper opportunity of giving some relief upon, it
> is, however, so very dangerous to be stirred that I trust everyone
> will see the propriety of not allowing it to be agitated on any
> account whatever.

It was probably the First Lord's last chance to scotch the mutiny.
But Spencer failed to take it: and before a year had passed,
*force majeure* had impelled him to change his tune altogether.
The worm was turning at last.

For already the yeast was at work, leavening the lump. No
one can say, of course, exactly when combination began, nor in
what ship. Yet it did begin to appear, and slowly spread from
ship to ship – very slowly indeed because communications between
the companies of ships were few and far between. For the men
*never* went ashore, on either long or short leave, since most of them,
if accorded this privilege, would never have returned. So there was
no chance at all of getting together in that way. The only chance
for inter-ship planning came when, on fine Sunday afternoons in
port, 'liberty-boats' – ironical name – were filled with the men
from different ships who rowed round the fleet asking – and receiving – such entertainment from any individual ship as its
abstinence could muster – quite lavish pint-pots of very indifferent
ship's beer or very small tots of rum saved out of the dinner-ration.

In fact it must have been on these rare Sunday visits that the organization necessary for any combination was built up.

The first stages of combination inside the individual ships must be left to the imagination. That was less remarkable, and fairly simply arranged since in all ships the whole company worked, fed and slept together on the Lower Deck. There was no privacy, of course, in the usually accepted sense of that word, but no doubt there were plenty of holes and corners into which one might creep in order to whisper into one's neighbour's ear without undue fear of being overheard by 'narks' (informers). Yet even so, it seems almost miraculous that all this early stage of whispering was completed without a single word of it reaching the narks' ears (and so the officers'). The reason, probably, why no news at all leaked out was the fact that on the Lower Deck at any time there must have been so many muffled curses, so many complaints just short of mutiny that they became hardly worth-while listening to, still less reporting. It is remarkable though, that no wolf in sheep's clothing ever succeeded in insinuating himself into the confidence of the bulk of the men. And this fact surely proves most convincingly that very nearly all the men must have been up to the neck in it.

Indeed, once the mutiny was under way, the unanimity of it was quite extraordinary. For there were in every ship a few evil souls who were constitutionally unable to combine with anyone. Such men were not, of course, of the old seaman-stock, who were notoriously as true as steel to each other. They were rather the earliest contributions from the Quota – impossible scamps from every slum in England; a kind of gaol-delivery of ne'er-do-wells, which the town authorities hastened gratefully to get rid of in their very first batches. The true seamen naturally knew these men of old, having been shipmates with them for some time. They would have nothing to do with them, and certainly did not entrust them with such perilous secrets.

Once the initial gaol-delivery was over, however, there arrived on shipboard, always in limited numbers, those other Quota-men already alluded to who, perhaps consciously, taught the old salt a lesson by instilling into his heart something very much like hope –

the information at any rate that his lot could be improved. Such men were certainly present in the fleet at Spithead in 1797; and their influence upon the majority was greater than their numbers.

There can be little doubt that the historian of the second – the Nore – mutiny is much better-placed than the one who tries to account for the Spithead affair. At the Nore, for instance, everyone knows that the ring-leader was one Richard Parker, and that he was both a relatively well-educated man and a Quota-man – though a closer examination does reveal the fact that he was by no means such a villain as he was painted at the time, and that, throughout, he was pushed into the leadership. But the astonishing thing about the Spithead Mutiny was that there were *no* ring-leaders – at least, if there were, we are by no means certain of their names. The whole thing was such a triumph of combination that it is quite impossible to spot the man who really led it. People have guessed, but they do not know. The man who usually has the distinction of being named first was a certain Valentine Joyce, a Quartermaster's Mate of the *Royal George*, and only twenty-six years old at the time. But it is almost a slur on a worthy character to call him ring-leader – a word which carries in ordinary life unpleasant overtones. There was, so far as we know, nothing unpleasant about Joyce – we know very little about him at all. So, if he deserves any name in connection with the mutiny, it is 'leader' – not 'ring-leader'. Furthermore, *if* he was leader, he was in his way the most consummate, the most brilliant, that ever emerged on the world's stage as leading any mutiny. For he so contrived it that he nowhere left any trace of his leadership behind, to catch any watchful eye which might be lying in wait for him. To the outward eye the whole mutiny was a perfect example of pure combination. Seeing that we are discussing an affair which was being conducted by a finite number of mortal men, we can but suppose that there was one of them who played a more leading part than the rest: and he, in everyday parlance, may be dubbed the leader of the mutiny. But – whether it was Valentine Joyce or someone else – he was much too clever to allow himself to be signalled out for the honour. And honour, in this author's view, it was. For it *is* an honour to have been the leader of so righteous a cause, and it is an honour to have conducted the whole thing with such outstanding skill.

The only leaders who are allowed at any given moment to appear as such were the thirty-two 'Delegates', two from each of the sixteen ships of the line in Spithead. They met in the Great Cabin – once Lord Howe's – of the *Queen Charlotte* on the first day of the uprising, and thereafter they met daily to control the whole thing. They and only they *appeared* as leaders, and their names of course are known. But their names are the only things we do know – their names and their ratings on board: and at first sight we may be surprised to learn that, far from being either firebrands or Quota-men, they were clearly sober, respectable men of the old seaman-class: and most were not even ratings – there were no ordinary seamen among their number and only thirteen Able Seamen. The rest were Petty Officers of one sort or another, including five Midshipmen – not the 'makee-learn' kind of Young Gentlemen on their way to commissioned rank, but the older kind of Lower Deck Midshipmen who had earned the rank by close attention to duty. (These men, as were all Midshipmen officially, were Petty Officers too.) It is quite possible that Valentine Joyce was in his origins a Quota-man, if only because his standard of education seems almost too high to make it likely that he was a true 'tarpaulin'. But even this is not certain.[1]

Perhaps the only man who – if he existed at all – *must* have been a Quota-man was a mysterious character called Evans, who had, some time in his life, been trained as a lawyer. (For there never probably was such a phenomenon as a trained lawyer among the true seamen.) But – oddly enough – the name of Evans does not figure in the known list of Delegates, though in fact he may well have been one, entered in the list under an assumed name. This Evans, in fact, may be said to exist only in the rather feverish imagination of various shore-based contemporary theorists, who thought he must exist because they could not understand how the mutiny could have happened without him. We find such witnesses

[1] He may possibly have been a 'Lord Mayor's Man', as it is suggested below that John Fleming may have been: but this too is only conjecture. See p. 148.

speaking with confidence about 'one Evans, an Attorney with a shady past, who had sought to escape the punishment he deserved by taking the Quota'. But that is literally all that we do know about him. Otherwise Evans totally escapes our vigilance, because we know neither the assumed name under which he masqueraded nor from which of the ships he was a Delegate. He is in fact just about as shadowy as he is shady; and he may well be a bogey-man of frightened rumour, and not a real person at all. He was surely not Joyce's fellow-Delegate from the *Royal George*. That was John Morrice, a tough Aberdonian A.B. of thirty-three years of age: and he was certainly not a Quota-man. Yet, though there may not have been many of them among the Delegates, their influence, especially in the early stages, must have been considerable. It is even quite possible that the Delegates themselves were only a façade, with the real leaders – Quota-men – acting as *éminences grises* in the background the whole time. For somebody – and relatively well-educated somebodies at that – must have instilled into the body of Delegates the will to look after the men's interests.

It is quite plain that, long before they met as Delegates, this body – however inspired – had been doing yeoman service throughout the fleet. Thus – though Heaven alone knows how – they had contrived to prepare no less than eleven petitions, each one written out separately, yet all obviously emanating from a common mind. And, by March 7, they had got them all despatched to Admiral Lord Howe, the titular Commander-in-Chief of the fleet, who was very popular throughout the Service. This old gentleman, now seventy-two years of age, was at Bath, being treated for gout. But the men firmly believed in their 'Black Dick' (as they called him) who had led many of them to victory on the First of June, three years before. They knew that he sympathized with the common man, and that he never failed when in command to visit the sick and maimed among them, or – if the worst came to the worst – to write letters of kindness to their next of kin. And now they had great – perhaps exaggerated – hopes that he would forward their petition to the Admiralty, and, by using his influence with them, ensure a favourable answer. They were not, they felt, asking more of him than they deserved, and the tone of their petition was

humility itself. Though each one was differently worded, the
following from the *Queen Charlotte* is typical of them all:

> 'To the Right Honourable Richard, Earl Howe, Admiral of the
> Fleet and General of Marines.
> The humble petitioners on board His Majesty's Ship *Queen
> Charlotte* on behalf of themselves and their brethren on board of
> the fleet at Spithead. Most humbly sheweth that your peti-
> tioners most humbly intreat that your Lordship would be pleased
> to take the hardships of which they complain into consideration
> and lay them before the Lords Commissioners of the Admiralty,
> not doubting in the least from your Lordship's interference in
> their behalf they will obtain a speedy redress.'
>
> 2. It is noticed that, two years ago, the pay of the Army and
>    Militia was raised, and that in consequence the seamen have
>    been expecting equal treatment,
> 3. they being fully as loyal to their Sovereign and as courageous
>    as any in His Majesty's service, 'as your Lordship can witness
>    who so often led them to victory and glory, and by whose
>    manly exertions the British Flag rides triumphant in every
>    quarter of the Globe'.
> 4. The last rise in wages took place in the reign of King Charles
>    II,[1] since when the cost of living has almost doubled, and the
>    cost of slops raised by 30 per cent.
> 5. 'Your petitioners relying on your goodness and benevolence
>    humbly implores that my Lords Commissioners of the
>    Admiralty will comply with the prayers of this petition, and
>    grant such addition will be made in their pay as in their Lord-
>    ships' wisdom they shall think meet. And your petitioners will
>    in duty bound ever pray, etc.'

Could anything be more reasonable? All they were asking, note, is
equality with the Army and the Militia. Nor were they guilty of
mutiny – yet. A 'humble petition' was perfectly legal, and both
common sense and humanity would suggest that, at the very least,

[1] Here they understated their case. The last rise was in January 1652–3,
in the time of the Commonwealth.

some sort of acknowledgement should have been made, even if no other notice was taken. Yet, so far as the men knew, nothing was done. And, in fact, nothing very much *was* done, even by Howe. Still, he did do something, even though he seems to have thought all eleven of the petitions were the work of one state-the-case malcontent who had cleverly disguised his handwriting. So perhaps no very great blame for what followed can be attached to him. He was a sick old man, longing for repose and feeling that he ought no longer to be bothered. But he did write to one of the junior Lords of the Admiralty, suggesting that, when next visiting Portsmouth, he should make a few tentative inquiries about whether anyone had noticed any special signs of discontent in the fleet. This was done, and the answer returned was a quite decisive 'No!' Lord Howe was relieved but not completely satisfied, for he was a conscientious old gentleman. So, on going up to Town on March 22, he handed all the petitions over to the same Admiralty Lord, who showed them at once to the First Lord. But that was as far as they went. The whole Board, considering them at its next meeting, concluded unanimously that nothing should be done about them. And nothing was – they were not even acknowledged.

The seamen's leaders were determined not to spoil everything by undue haste. Although the men were, not unnaturally, expecting some result, daily growing more and more impatient when no answer came, they restrained everybody's frustration until April 16, and then gave the word. The mutiny was on. But even then they would have waited for a day or two longer, had not a rumour somehow reached the ears of certain officers that disaffection was afoot: and the leaders were so anxious that the plot should not go off at half-cock that they ordered an instant start. From their angle, however, all was well. Though bustled at the last moment, they did succeed in seeing to it that everyone in the fleet obeyed their firm lead. And what a feat that was! The average crews of the 1790s contained every description of individual, good and bad, as one may well imagine. And all were made successfully to toe the line:

old tars, young sailors, sturdy loyalists, seditious malcontents from Ireland or elsewhere, pressed men, volunteers, gaol-birds,

men of no education, and Quota-men of more than a little;
there were escaping debtors and honest men; there were men
you could trust mingled with thieves and card-sharpers whom
to trust with a chew of tobacco would be folly; and to increase
the difficulty there were ten per cent of foreigners.[1]

And – somehow – all these diverse elements were welded together
by those nameless leaders into one impenetrable and unshakable
whole. With one accord every man of them kept faith: none failed.
It is, to this day, truly amazing.

Yet, still, there was only the one act of mutiny. It was mutiny
when, spontaneously, every man on board refused to weigh
anchor. But for a long time there was no other illegality committed. For the officers could do nothing but acquiesce in the
orders of their new masters – the Delegates who now met daily
in the Great Cabin of the *Queen Charlotte*. These same men were
scrupulously polite. Orders were issued to the men that they should
carry on outwardly as before, paying their customary respect to the
officers, and obeying their orders in every particular save just the
one – that no attention was to be paid to the order of 'Weigh
Anchor'. The Delegates also took over the duty of enforcing
discipline. When, for instance, a rating of the *Pompée* brought
liquor on board contrary to the Delegates' orders, he was seized
up to the gangway and given a dozen with the cat on the bare back
by the Boatswain's mates. The honours invariably paid to the
Captains on leaving or on entering their ships were still scrupulously
preserved. But now the Delegates were accorded the same
honours. When they came or went the side-boys rigged side-
ropes to the gangways; the men fell in, the Marine Guard turned
out; the Boatswain 'piped the side' both for the Captain and for the
Delegates. In fact, now, the only difference between Captain and
Delegate was that the commissioned officers were not asked to
turn out in force to greet the Delegates, as they always greeted the
Captain.

The Delegates, too, were uncannily wise in their dealings with
the nation as a whole; for from the first they meant to get, and to

[1] B. Dobrée and G. E. Manwaring, *The Floating Republic*, 1935, p. 17.

keep, the sympathy and good opinion of the country, and especially of the great merchants. They therefore ordained that only the ships of the line should fight in the seamen's interests. The smaller ships whose duty was normally to protect British trade were to continue to do so in the ordinary way. At first they had some difficulty with certain of the frigates and sloops at Spithead who were anxious to stop there and see the fun. But the Delegates' word was law, and any recalcitrant small ship soon found itself looking down the run-out guns of two sail of the line: which rough argument in turn soon got frigate or sloop to sea and engaged on its usual commerce-protecting chores. It was at this moment, too, that the leaders solemnly announced that, if news were brought that the French fleet had put to sea, the big ships themselves would up-anchor at once and, putting themselves under their officers again, would postpone their quarrel with the Admiralty until the enemy was dealt with. It was such moves as these which instantly won for the fleet the sympathy and good will of the greater part of the public, for it was evident to the man in the street, even when quite uninformed, that people who were prepared to carry on with all essential duties could not possibly be blood-thirsty mutineers.

The Delegates reinforced their demands by sending a petition – still very humble and very legal – to Parliament. It began – as did the original petition to Lord Howe – with the request for more pay. But now it went a good deal further, and introduced several more of the men's grievances.

The first of these was about the quantity and quality of their food. They demanded that the 14-ounce pound should go, and that better comestibles should be provided. They even ventured to suggest that they should be served with fresh meat when in port, and an adequate supply of vegetables. Next, they declared that the sick on board should always receive proper medical attention, and that such invalid stores as were allowed should always be forthcoming and not, as often happened, be embezzled. Next came a very revolutionary suggestion – that ordinary leave should be allowed to the fleet when in harbour. They knew very well, of course, why it had never been granted – because forcible recruitment made it unlikely that many would return at the end of it. So they themselves proposed a system of bounds beyond which liberty-men should not be allowed to go. The fifth section of the petition contained two separate demands: the first – one of their most crying grievances – was that any man wounded in action should continue to be paid his wages until cured, instead of having them stopped until such time as he reported for duty again (for that had always been the truly skin-flint policy of the Administration). The second was a general demand; and it perhaps asked as much as all the rest put together. All they said was, 'if any ship has real grievances to complain of, we hope Your Lordships will readily redress them, as far as is in your power, to prevent disturbances'. What they meant – and what the Authorities knew they meant – was a demand to be listened to if brutally bullied by their officers.

At first sight it is strange, but it is none the less true, that at no time did the mutineers mention flogging, or any other kind of corporal punishment, as a thing which ought to be abolished in the Navy, despite the fact that it was notorious throughout the Service that the punishments were sometimes too brutal for words, and that some of the officers ought to have been ashamed of their senseless cruelty. The fact is indeed far otherwise. The men expressed their *approval* of flogging as an institution. The seamen among them knew only too well the many criminal types which had recently found their way on to the Lower Deck, and they knew that the power to order 'a dozen at the gangway' was one of the greatest protections to honest men. In a word, it was not flogging that they objected to, but excessive flogging. The sea-man-element in this, as in every other respect, showed itself to be very sensible and well-balanced. It was a *general* protection from brutal officers that they were asking in the last clause of their petition.

Meanwhile, roused at last to the dangers of the situation, Spencer decided to go down to Portsmouth in person, accompanied by some of his colleagues. They arrived at midday on April 18, and instantly summoned Lord Bridport and his subordinate Admirals, Gardner, Colpoys and Pole, to attend him and to give him their latest report. Then, still failing entirely to appreciate the situation, and the unyielding determination of the fleet, they composed what they called a 'project', in which they offered a few shillings more pay to the various ratings, but practically nothing else. On the quality and the quantity of food there was silence; the request for fresh meat and vegetables was ignored; and treatment of the sick, leave while in port, and pay for the wounded were not mentioned. Nor, of course, was there anything about the individual grievances either. And the unfortunate Admirals were instructed to put this 'project' before the Delegates.

The Admirals, of course, obeyed; but naturally the Delegates were not at all enthusiastic about the 'project'. Hour after hour they sat in their Great Cabin, their opposition gradually hardening as the hours went by. Meanwhile Their Lordships, utterly convinced that the answer when it came from the *Queen Charlotte* would take the form of an unconditional surrender, sat down to a good dinner. It was not until 4.30 on the 19th that the Delegates' answer reached them. It was quite polite, but it was ominously firm – it simply repeated the demands made in the Parliamentary petition, omitting nothing and adding nothing – except that the wages they were demanding were now stated exactly – one shilling a day for all A.B.s. My Lords were furious. Fortified by their dinner with its fine wines, they voted forthwith that the rascals must give way, and accept what their liberality had offered. They even concocted a bold plan for luring most of the ships down to St Helens, leaving only the worst ones at Spithead. Then they went to bed, having commanded Lord Bridport and his Admirals to attend in the morning.

In the chilly light of day, however, their plans of the preceding evening looked a good deal less rosy, especially when, with cold common sense, the Admirals with one accord pointed out their stark impossibility. *Every man in the fleet,* they said, was of one way of thinking. Not a hand would be raised to get up an anchor. The only thing to do now was for Their Lordships to give way! It was straight talk from the Admirals to the Admiralty.

Thus deserted by the men on the spot, who clearly knew what they were talking about, Spencer now gave a good deal of ground, though still far from all. The Delegates' pay demands for the seamen were to be fully met: so was the 16-ounce pound. But nothing else. That, he still verily believed, would be enough; and all the Captains in the fleet were ordered instantly to summon their men and make them accept the new terms.

This they did on the 21st; and some of them – the more popular and/or the more eloquent ones – came within an ace of success. Captain Holloway of the *Duke,* for instance, all but got his men to return to duty – and perhaps would have done so had not a voice at the back of the assembled seamen cried at the critical moment, 'Let us wait and hear what the *Queen Charlottes* say!' And this great feeling of loyalty to their leaders ultimately prevailed in every ship. Then Admiral Gardner, a brave and eloquent officer, determined to try again on his own. So he had himself rowed to the *Queen Charlotte* – his own ship was the *Royal Sovereign* – in order to address the whole body of Delegates together. And such was his power of persuasion that for a long time he came near to success. But at last he too was thwarted, this time by the return of Joyce and Morrice who had not heard his elegant language. Those careful souls did not like the Admiralty's insistence upon the theme of 'forgiveness', with its implication that the men had done something which needed it: and they persuaded the rest without much difficulty that only one thing could make them all safe from subsequent punishment, and that was the King's Royal Pardon. At this Gardner got very cross, losing his temper and shouting, and even threatening violence to one of the Delegates. But from such folly he was saved by being politely but firmly shown to the ship's gangway and forced to leave the *Queen Charlotte.*

The Delegates then held council again, and produced a new answer. No verbal message brought to them by anybody would be acceptable. Nothing but an Act of Parliament would do now, succinctly naming as granted all their demands. On top of this, too, there must now be a full Royal Pardon. Actually, that Royal Pardon was of prime importance to them. In the recent case of the *Culloden,* the leaders had thought themselves pardoned: but they had found out their mistake too late, when they could not produce the necessary evidence which would have saved their necks.

This had taught them the perils of naval rebellion, and that mutineers must make no mistakes nor take anything for granted. This new message was now sent, and it concluded with these determined words – 'and this is the total and final answer'. Moreover Lord Spencer, when he read it, seems to have decided that he must give way, and that he might as well do now what he would be forced to do later. Though it was now midnight, he instantly got into his carriage and started out to obtain the Royal Pardon. Spencer was no fool. He even knew when to give way with the best possible grace.

While he was away, there came an interval of several days in which not much progress was made either way. The public press and the people of Portsmouth (many of whom had relatives among the men in the fleet) were already beginning to take the thing comparatively light-heartedly. Indeed there was now a touch of comic relief, which raised a good-humoured laugh all round. It chanced just then that the Prince of Württemberg, who was in England at that time a-courting the Princess Royal, was due to go to Portsmouth to receive the freedom of the City: and, for his amusement, he was to be received by Lord Bridport in the Commissioner's barge, who was to take him for a trip round the fleet at Spithead. The whole programme was punctually fulfilled, though every ship was still in open mutiny. What is more, eye witnesses tell us, as the Commissioner's barge drew alongside each ship, the mutineers manned the yards and gave the royal visitor three lusty cheers!

They were like that. Circumstances may have made them mutineers for the moment, but they regarded themselves as honest Englishmen, with honest English feelings. They liked manning the yards: they liked paying their respects to visiting V.I.P.s. But – let anyone at his peril think otherwise! –

They would obey orders with alacrity, they would treat their officers with respect, but they would not forget. Outwardly restrained, they were simmering underneath. Yet in this period of uneasy waiting the leaders kept absolute control, for they possessed faculties which very seldom go together – the capacity

141

to work the feelings of the men up to a state of revolt, combined with the power to direct the course of events after the first explosion. They seem to have judged with almost perfect precision how far they could go; but the old life, they swore, would never come back: they had had enough.[1]

How one would have liked to meet the real leaders, and to study their personalities at close quarters!

Lord Spencer soon secured the King's Royal Pardon, had a hundred copies of it printed, and sent them down to Spithead. Bridport now addressed the crew of his flagship, the *Royal George,* who lowered the Red Flag of Mutiny and ran up the C-in-C's. And even the men of the *Queen Charlotte,* including the Delegates, after a more careful scrutiny of the Pardon, professed themselves satisfied, and once more manned the yards, this time in token of return to duty. The next morning many of the fleet dropped down to St Helens, and during the next four days most of the rest joined them. It looked to everyone as though the 'Breeze' was over.

And so it would have been, had the authorities behaved with a modicum of good sense. They knew now – or certainly should have known – that the men had had their deepest suspicions aroused: and at all costs they should have busied themselves in allaying them. It was obviously a case not only for doing right, but for letting the men see that right was being done. For now another danger arose – which must be partly laid at the door of the men themselves. They were basically ignorant, uneducated people, and so they probably did not appreciate the amount of time which is necessary before the cumbrous constitutional machinery of parliamentary procedure can be set in motion. To them a few broad strokes of the legislator's pen should have done their business for them. But, though legislation is never quite so simple as that, even yet the lawyers and the Members of Parliament had quite failed to realize that haste was still of the essence. So the Government wasted time – not perhaps deliberately, and certainly not treacherously – by appointing statutory committees to look into the proposals, and by generally havering around in their customary way

[1] Dobrée and Manwaring, op. cit. p. 66.

until the inevitable happened. The seamen, suspicious and sulky, began to sense treachery where none was designed. It must be admitted, too, that at this juncture the Admiralty experienced cruel hard luck in the weather. If only the wind had come fair, the fleet at St Helens could, and would, have sailed, and none of the ships' companies would have been able to continue their carefully-prepared combination, But the wind remained foul, cooping them all up in St Helens.

So the men grew daily more and more impatient: nor did the Admiralty help in its rather blunt and even surly communications with the men; nor indeed in its ability to produce at a moment's notice the (to them) unaccustomed stocks of fresh meat and fresh vegetables. Doubtless such luxuries were difficult to produce out of a hat at any given moment: but there are ways and means of doing things, and the Admiralty's way was certainly not the happiest. In fine, the men became more and more convinced that they were being sold down the river, especially when a garbled version of a House of Lords debate appeared in the papers of May 3. So it came about that, on the 5th, a bundle of newspapers was thrown into the *Queen Charlotte* from the *Mars,* with a message which alleged outright that Parliament was on the point of throwing out the Seamen's Bill. In vain did Bridport try to show that the Bill was going forward as fast as possible. Then a rumour started in the *Duke* that her Captain, Holloway, had received a sinister order from the Admiralty; and the crew insisted on seeing it. If he ever had any such order, he now said that he had destroyed it; whereupon the men, goaded to desperation by their fears, laid violent hands on him and threatened him with a flogging, if not with death. On that occasion they recovered their natural poise in time, and did not proceed to extremes. It was none the less raw, red mutiny, and it was not the last case of its kind.

On May 7 the wind changed, and the fleet could have put to sea. But by that time it was prepared to do no such thing. The seamen, once more and unanimously, refused to budge.

So it was rebellion again, and a good deal more dangerous this time than it had been before. For the men now felt themselves to be duped, though in fact they were not, and their mood was savage. It was now, for the first time – and, in Spithead, fortunately the last – that blood was shed in the fleet.

It happened in the *London*, the flagship of Admiral Sir John Colpoys: and, if it is possible to pin-point a culprit, it was probably the Admiral himself. His Captain, Griffith (who was also his nephew), reported to him as he lay in Spithead on the 7th, that the Delegates' boats were coming up from St Helens to visit the 'hard cases' (of which the *Mars* was one) which were still lying at the main anchorage. Then, in an ill moment for everybody, Colpoys lost his temper, saying roundly that he would no longer tolerate these mutinous dogs. This time, Lord Bridport was not near by to restrain him, and he decided to prevent the Delegates from entering his ship. He began by having all hands turned up on deck, where, having addressed them, he somehow came to the fatal conclusion that they would obey him if he were to issue positive orders. He therefore had all his boats hoisted in, and he sent the men below with strict instructions to shut the port-lids, thus keeping the Delegates out. It was a dangerous move – to try and drive a wedge between leaders and men until he was quite sure of his own control. And at first it seemed that all was going to be well, because most of the men obeyed; but not quite all, some of them remaining on the forecastle. In spite of this, however, he still persisted on his course, had the hatches which led below closed and armed his officers and marines. It was the men on the forecastle who spoilt his plan, for, throughout, they could see what the Admiral was doing.

The Delegates reached the *London* and were warned off by the sentries. But the main body of the seamen, shut in below hatches, very soon became unruly and tried to open them, only to be confronted by the armed officers. These, before firing, asked Colpoys for instructions – were they to fire, in order to keep the ship's company below-deck? And Colpoys replied, 'Yes!' At this – and before anyone fired – the hands on the forecastle began to unlash a gun situated there, to haul it round and cover the officers. Thereupon, Peter Bover, the ship's First Lieutenant, warned them that he would fire unless they desisted. Such was Bover's hold over them that all but one man did desist: but that one went on

18. Seaspeed (British Rail) hovercraft at Portsmouth Harbour Station.
Spithead can be seen through the Harbour entrance between Portsmouth
Point and Fort Blockhouse

19. Portsmouth Regatta, 1827. On the right, the Earl of Belfast's *Therese* is beating Thomas Assheton Smith's *Menai*. On the left, *Pearl*

boldly clearing the piece. So Bover fired, hitting the man and mortally wounding him. It was for long believed that the dead man was one of the *London*'s Delegates: but such was not the case.

At once the cry arose of 'blood for blood!' The men on the forecastle surged towards the quarterdeck, the men below stormed the hatches, the officers fired to keep them back, and in a moment the fighting became general, several on both sides being wounded, including a Delegate, and three seamen killed. But almost at once the marines changed sides, their allegiance from the first being very doubtful. As soon as Colpoys saw this he recovered his senses, and quickly realized that he must accept defeat before the exchange of bullets became general. Some of the steadier men too interposed to try and prevent further bloodshed, and hostilities ended very soon after they had begun. But the situation remained horribly tense. Lieutenant Bover had already been seized, and hauled forward on to the forecastle, where a yard-rope was rove and the noose adjusted round his neck. And it would have gone ill with him but for the timely intervention of one of the Delegates from another ship who had somehow clambered on board. This was none other than Valentine Joyce, the *Royal George* Delegate. So here we see for the first time this twenty-six-year old leader in the very act of leading. He certainly showed no indecision. He rushed up to Bover, put his arm round his neck and shouted as loud as he could above the tumult of sound, 'If you hang this young man, you shall hang me, for I shall never quit him!' Whereupon one of the *London*'s topmen added his voice to the din, declaring loudly that Bover was 'a brave boy'. Then, while the executioners still hesitated, Admiral Colpoys himself pushed his way into the mêlée shouting – which was only the truth – that he, having given the order to fire, was the only one really to blame. It was an exciting moment, and it shows up the principal actors in a very pleasing light. Moreover its sequel was quite as pleasing and even more unexpected. Imagine seven or eight hundred men in the last stages of frenzy, covering with their trigger-happy fingers one intrepid flag officer. Suddenly – from the wings, as it were, of the swirling multitude – a hoarse voice was heard to shout, 'You're a damned bloody scoundrel!'

But this alone proved more than the men could stomach. What a wonderful thing is ingrained habit, the custom of a lifetime! Far from continuing their threats to Colpoys, as one man the ratings turned upon the hoarse-voiced one, saying in effect, 'how dare *you* speak like that to a *British Admiral*?' – and they threatened then and there to give him a flogging – and did give him a ducking. This episode instantly reduced the tension, and the men allowed Colpoys to have his say with comparatively few interruptions. He exonerated Bover altogether and half-excused himself on the grounds of his latest orders from the Admiralty. The men insisted upon seeing them, which gave the Admiral the opportunity to lower the temperature still further by spending a long time looking for them. When at last he showed them, he saw, with who knows what relief, that they had removed the halter from Bover's neck. The men now pocketed their fire-arms: but they led Colpoys, Griffith and Bover away to their cabins, and locked them in under close arrest. And, instead of the Admiral's usual banner, they hoisted at the mast-head the Red Flag.

Bover, one of the involuntary heroes of this strange epic – the only letting of blood during the whole Spithead Mutiny – would appear at first sight to be lucky in escaping a violent death. He was not so much lucky, however, as deserving; and the real reason why he was not hanged outright on that occasion was because he had always made himself very popular with the men of the *London*, being a young man with definite ideas on maintaining discipline among them: not by starting with a rope's end, but by gaining their confidence. And as one reads accounts of this mutiny, with their inevitable stress on starting, flogging and bullying, it is rather too easy, unless one is careful, to conclude that most officers were in varying degrees unintelligent sadists, unworthy of the name of Britons. It is true that there were such people, and more of them than was good for the Service: but it is equally true that the majority of naval officers, junior as well as senior, were much more like the fairminded Peter Bover.

This time the Delegates had come to Spithead with two clear objects in view. The first was to see that the authorities did not weaken them by trying to separate them. It is doubtful whether their Lordships were really being so Machiavellian: there is no reason for supposing that, after their original climb-down, they were intent on behaving unfairly – they were only moving ludicrously slowly. Their second object was to get the more unpopular officers out of the ships, thus presenting their somewhat vague point about 'grievances' to the Admiralty as a *fait accompli*. Thus, in this sort of gaol-delivery-in-reverse the Delegates got rid of well over 100 officers, who were packed off to the shore with varying degrees of contumely and in varying numbers from the different ships. Thus the *Glory* lost every single one of her officers. From the *Duke* they made Captain Holloway depart. Twenty-one others went too, but against the names of six of them a cross was inserted, which meant that, when happier days returned, they might come back to the ship.

Meanwhile the great talking-point all over the country was what the mutineers would do with Colpoys, Griffith and Bover, now hauled before a regular Tribunal set up in the *Queen Charlotte* by order of the Delegates. They were, it was known, to be court martialled on the charge of murder. What everyone was asking was whether the Delegates would dare to convict them, and still more to execute them if convicted. But this was hardly the point. The Delegates had already shown that they would dare anything. There were, however, as they had so often proved, some very wise heads among them, and these would no doubt see the dangers of shedding any more blood, especially that of senior officers. What, they must have asked themselves anxiously, would be the effect upon the country if they took the life, say, of Admiral Colpoys? They knew they must retain the sympathy of the whole people: and would public opinion condone an offence like that? Yet for a long time it was touch and go how the court would decide. The feeling against the prisoners – and especially against the Admiral – was still very bitter: and there was a powerful lobby among the men which urged that 'blood must have blood'. In fact what in the end brought down the scales in favour of clemency was the speech of the last-appointed Delegate of all – a certain John Fleming who had only just taken the place of the one wounded in the *London* fracas. This young man was an Able Seaman of only 25 years of age. Fortunately the speech he made to the court has come down to us complete; it shows a very wise head on such young shoulders – and a very eloquent tongue too. It would be interesting to know more about Fleming. He does not sound like one of the common run of seamen – he could express himself altogether too well for that. He may, of course, have been a Quota-man, though these as a rule were rather older. Was he, then, possibly one of that rather rare fraternity known in their own day as 'My Lord Mayor's Men'? These were young bloods of various kinds (but often well-born) who had fallen foul of the watch in London, and who had been shipped off into the fleet without many questions being asked or answered – often to save good family names from shame or embarrassment. Admittedly such young ne'er-do-wells did not as a rule make good, but John Fleming may have been an exception, for he was certainly a well-educated man with a logical mind: and if at this crisis in his life he had had the good fortune to fall into good company, or even come under the influence of a good man, surely anything might be possible. It is certainly only a fancy to assume it: but it is at least on the cards that that good man was Peter Bover, Fleming's First Lieutenant in the *London*, of whom in his statement he speaks with approval amounting almost to affection.

Had they [the ship's company of the *London*] followed the momentary impulse of passion, and wreaked their vengeance on that unfortunate gentleman, a few minutes would have brought to their recollection the amiable character he always bore among them, and I am convinced would have embittered the latest moment of their lives . . . and before this hand shall subscribe the name of Fleming to anything that may in the least tend to that gentleman's prejudice, much more his life, I will undergo your utmost violence, and meet death with him hand in hand.

This eloquent plea prevailed, as it richly deserved, and orders were at once sent to the *London* that Bover should be released. He *was* released, but he did not leave the ship. The men did not even suggest that he should: in fact they urged him to stay. So he remained on board until the following spring, when he was promoted to the rank of Commander and given his own ship. He was made Post in 1800, but did not live long enough to reach his Flag.

Colpoys and Griffith, too, were ultimately acquitted by the Tribunal, but not nearly so handsomely as Bover. Both were sent ashore, and Colpoys was never again given another command, even by the Admiralty, who found they could not approve his action in the *London*. Griffith, however, who later took the name of Colpoys, received his Flag in due course and did fly it at sea. Perhaps the Admiral's personal bravery deserved a better fate, but he had certainly acted irresponsibly in challenging the men as he did.

Before leaving this episode, it is worth remarking that a strong factor in the men's dealings with Bover was probably developed when an inquest was held at Haslar Hospital on the bodies of the shot men, and the Lieutenant was called as a witness. After discussion between the Delegates, he was allowed to go ashore on his promise to return to the ship. The Coroner returned a verdict of 'justifiable homicide'. It was urged on Bover by his friends that the promise given under duress was not binding; but he held that he was bound to return, and return he did, to the cheers of his mutineer shipmates.

The burial of the dead mutineers was as remarkable as the rest of the affair. The men wished to bury their comrades in the graveyard of St Mary's, the parish church of Portsea, and to do so with some ceremony. The Military Governor of Portsmouth was violently against admitting any number of mutineers to Portsmouth or Portsea, and was on the verge of starting a private war of Britain's premier Naval Port versus Britain's Royal Navy – a battle bound to be a dead loss to Britain, whoever won. He even mounted braziers on a battery beside the Square Tower at the bottom of the High Street in order to prepare red-hot shot for bombarding the ships, an event still commemorated in the name of these ramparts – the Hot Walls. However, the Mayor, Sir John Carter, the most notable of a dynasty of Carter Mayors, made himself responsible with another magistrate, Mr Godwin the banker, for escorting the cortège through the town.

There are two versions of what happened after the funeral. Mr Midshipman Symonds, who was later to be Admiral Sir William Symonds, Surveyor of the Navy and designer of Queen Victoria's steam yacht *Victoria and Albert I*, said that the mourners all returned drunk and were heavily punished by the Delegates. On the other hand, a descendant of Captain Giffard, son-in-law of Sir John Carter, recounts the story that, when all the mourners were soberly aboard the boats ready to go off to their ships, two of the Delegates returned to the Mayor's house to thank him for his protection. Sir John then took the opportunity of asking for news of Admiral Colpoys. One of the Delegates was from the *London* and replied that he was well enough at present. Was he a friend of the Mayor? Yes, replied Sir John, and added that he hoped no ill would befall him. Both Delegates replied that none should. They kept their word. Next day they lowered the gig, the fastest boat in the ship, bustled the Admiral into it, and raced for the shore, hotly pursued by the boats of the more militant *Mars*. They lay-to off the Sallyport under the protection of the guns and demanded to speak to the Mayor, to whom they handed over the Admiral against the Mayor's written promise to produce him for trial in a Court of Justice when called upon to do so. Admiral Colpoys considered that he owed his life to Sir John, and, when he returned to London, he told the King so. In fact it seems most unlikely that the Delegates, who had at this stage already acquitted the Admiral, would have now harmed a hair of his head; but the story is a pleasing one.

The blood shed in the *London* scared everybody, and at last taught the authorities that procrastination was perilous. So, on May 8, the Seamen's Bill came up in the Commons, not as a Statute in its own right but as a financial resolution, which no one was now in the mood to question. Charles James Fox, the Leader of the Opposition, had a fine field day with his outspoken criticism of the Government's conduct of the affair, but the thing went through both Houses without a hitch and received the Royal Assent the same day.

But now a fresh Royal Pardon had become necessary – at least the men refused to return to duty until it arrived. However,

Royal Pardons were the easiest part of the business, and a new one couched in the widest possible terms was at once issued. Then came the question of how best to wind up the whole distressing business tactfully. And somebody – either Pitt or the King himself – had an ingenious brain-wave. The mutiny should be ended in pageantry, and the key-figure in that pageant should be none other than old Lord Howe. He could – and would – do the job well: not only because he was the Old Hero, but also (it must be admitted) because he was still a little ashamed of his conduct over the petitions. So, when invited to step forward, he wound himself up to a prodigious effort for so gout-ridden an old gentleman, and accepted the task. What he undertook was no child's play for the aged Admiral. He was to visit every ship in the fleet separately, and in each he was to talk, heart to heart as it were, with his beloved 'children'. This full programme was carried out. He still had their hearts, and the whole experiment was the greatest success.

The climax was arranged for the Sunday – which, characteristically, dawned with a fog over Spithead through which, at first, nothing at all was visible. But the day relented as the sun gained power, and by ten o'clock it had cleared sufficiently for spectators to see the Delegates, rowing in boats 'in two lines in great regularity', making for the guardship, the *Royal William* – that well-known antique now over a century old. Lord Howe was there, and he was punctually and punctiliously saluted by the Delegates. To complete the picture, Lady Howe was present too. Then Valentine Joyce, on behalf of all the Delegates, gallantly asked the honour of her company in their aquatic procession. She replied, graciously, that she had no fear, and would readily be of the party, whereupon Lord Howe, quite informally, invited Joyce into the Governor's House to 'take a glass of wine with him'. Joyce accepted this invitation, with no trace of awkwardness in his manner – he was, by now at any rate, a very collected young man. But, so far as one can see, he was not at all spoilt by his time as a Delegate. When all was over, it seems, he settled down again to his old post of quartermaster's mate in the *Royal George*. And at last, on May 17, with everything forgiven and forgotten, the Channel fleet put to sea.

Every single demand of the mutineers had been met – at least, if not granted immediately, accepted in principle and in due time implemented. It was certainly a wonderful triumph for combination and moreover it was virtually bloodless – for the solitary fracas in the *London* had been, as it were, incidental to the whole thing. While the excitement was at its hottest, many people in Great Britain, unwilling to believe that combination alone should have wrought such great results, had alleged that revolutionary influences must have been at work in the fleet – that, at the very least, the United Irishmen were busy fermenting trouble, even if pure Jacobinism from across the Channel was not at the root of things. So it is interesting to know that the Government itself instituted some searching inquiries to discover what deleterious foreign interests (if any) were present at Spithead. At about the time, therefore, that Lord Howe was paying his pacific visit to Portsmouth, an enterprising young magistrate called Aaron Graham was told to ferret out anything that would throw any light on this question. He was remarkably thorough and enjoyed his sleuthing no end: he tackled not only very nearly all the Delegates personally, but also (when he could get at them) their wives (yes, and their sweethearts and their mothers too). Finally, he concluded that he had laid bare the whole conspiracy, and found – just no conspiracy at all: that there was *no* force behind the Delegates save only the hitherto unrealized power of combination.

This is why the Spithead Mutiny remains such a landmark in British history, and especially in the history of British trade unionism. The Delegates at Spithead were among the earlier, if not the very earliest, exemplars of trade union leaders – and most accomplished ones at that. After all, does it not follow as night follows day? If the majority of the 'operatives' – whether workmen or seamen – decide unanimously to withhold their labour, and are intelligently led by competent union officials, what can 'the Management' (whether manufacturers, naval officers or Admiralty) do about it? In truth, nothing except give way with what grace they may!

The famous 'Breeze' at Spithead was not the only nor the last outbreak of mutiny in 1797. It had the support of the fleet at

Plymouth, and, even while the old Admiral was hob-nobbing with the young Delegate in Portsmouth, a much nastier affair was brewing at the Nore anchorage in the Thames. As a result, the North Sea fleet (including the ships at Yarmouth) came out at almost exactly the same moment as the Channel fleet went back to work. Moreover before the year was out there were several other rebellions – at the Cape, in the East Indies and at Cadiz. And, lastly, an infinitely nastier affair took place on board His Majesty's ship *Hermione* in the West Indies in September. Here an inhuman Captain paid for his inhumanity with his life, murdered with almost all his officers by a maddened crew. But a case like that was already becoming an exception after the 'Breeze' – indeed because of the 'Breeze'; because thereafter and for ever more the British seaman had earned his emancipation, and was no longer a slave. It is true he did not achieve total emancipation in one fell swoop. But undoubtedly the beginning of it all was at Spithead in April 1797.

On the other hand, the mutiny at the Nore was, by comparison, unnecessary, since all the really crying grievances had been attended to at Spithead; and it was conducted in an infinitely less satisfactory way. At one time, for instance, the better part of half the fleet was all lined up to sail away in a body for an enemy port. This alone was far more serious than anything which happened in the earlier mutiny, and it follows inevitably that order was restored only after the use of far more severity. It ended, in fact, in quite a blood-bath of official punishments. We are not concerned here with its details, but certain figures will show, if they reveal nothing else, the merits which accrue from sensible and orderly leadership.

As a result of the 'Breeze' no mutineer was court martialled: none was imprisoned and none flogged (save for a few punished by the Delegates themselves): none sentenced to death, and none hanged. At the Nore the figures were: tried by court martial, 412; imprisoned, 29; flogged, 9; sentenced to death, 59; executed, 29.

But perhaps the full difference is realized by remembering that Richard Parker dangled from the yard-arm of the *Sandwich,* but Valentine Joyce took wine with Lord Howe at Government House.

# Chapter VII

# ROYAL YACHTS, VISITS AND REVIEWS

The fighting ships of England have always been intimately associated with the Crown. Indeed, up to and including the time of Charles I they were the actual property of the Sovereign, built with his (or her) own money to his own specification, and usable – in theory – for his (or her) own purposes. Of such a sort was the Navy of Henry VII, who personally used his ships for trading and also hired them out to his merchant subjects. To his son, Henry VIII, his – 'the King's' – ships were particularly dear. All his life he took the greatest interest in them, in their build, in their armaments and in their numbers. He was proud of them, and delighted in showing them off to the various foreign royalties who visited him.

He went further than this, however, even going to the surprisingly modern length of holding a review of them, the very first of its kind at Spithead. (To date, the last was held in 1969: but we shall come to that all in good time.) The chronicler Holinshed narrates how the King in 1512, 'having a desire to see his Navy together, rode to Portsmouth', where he first assembled his Captains and then, having treated them to a banquet, had himself rowed round the anchored ships. It was a long time before this idea of a parade of ships occurred again. It was perhaps rather an expensive luxury so long as the Crown had to shoulder the burden of their upkeep; for there was little or no money in a review, and there were more remunerative things for his ships to do on those relatively few occasions when they were assembled into fleets.

By 1514, it is clear, the King had his own special ship called the

*Katherine Pleasaunce* – a small vessel of 100 tons burden which was laid down at Deptford. She was too small for the purposes of war, so very likely she was the first craft to which the name 'Royal Yacht' can be given. We do not know exactly where he went in her, nor even if he ever visited Spithead in her. But we do know that he used to visit his own fleet and his own ships. Such occasions furnished good opportunities for the monarch to dispense his patronage and to reward good services. And such visits happened quite often in Henry's time. Indeed, first and last, the King spent a great deal of time at Portsmouth and in its company – in 1545, for instance, when, as we saw, he was virtually the Navy's Commander-in-Chief, though he left the actual bother of going to sea to his Admiral Lord Lisle. After 1512, though, so far as is known, he did not *review* his fleet again.

Nor, when her time came, did his daughter Elizabeth, though her interest in 'the Queen's Ships' was very considerable indeed. In her day, however, the chief homes of her ships were in the Thames Estuary, and with these we are not primarily concerned here. Nor, probably, did she ever embark upon a sea voyage in her life, though every year she thought it her duty to go on a land 'progress' about the country. Though it is on record that, once, she got as far from Town, and as near to Portsmouth, as Southampton, it is more than doubtful whether she ever set eyes on the glittering waters of Spithead. It is a pity. One would like to see in one's mind's eye the Virgin Queen on the quarterdeck of one of her ships anchored off Portsmouth, perhaps giving the accolade of knighthood to one of her seamen officers. But such a view would not be founded upon history. Drake, it is true, was so honoured by her. But the scene of the episode was Deptford, not Portsmouth. Again, John Hawkins, Martin Frobisher and several more were knighted at sea for their services against the Armada; however, the place was not Spithead but the Channel somewhere between Wight and Calais; nor did the Queen perform the ceremony herself, but left it to her deputy, the Lord Admiral Howard of Effingham.

Her successor, the rather unattractive James I, did not have the interest in ships which had characterized his predecessors; but he did get his ship-builder Phineas Pett to build a little 25-footer for his son, Prince Henry, a gallant boy who got to love both the little boat (not yet known as a yacht) and its builder. This promising youth, however, died before his father, which was a great loss to his country. It is also recorded that James did once go to Portsmouth, to view some of his ships – that squadron which had carried his son Charles, the new heir, and his favourite, Buckingham, to Spain and back again on a fool's mission. There is no evidence, though, that he made himself popular with either the officers or the men in that fleet.

Charles I, his son, was of course very different from his father. An artist at heart, he always loved, and took an artist's interest in, his tall ships. Incidentally, he caused to be built the tallest of them, the greatest ship up to that time ever to grace the Royal Navy, the famous *Sovereign of the Seas*. And he watched her building with almost fatherly affection. But that was at Chatham. Nor is there any evidence that he ever had a yacht of his own. Yet one of the naval expeditions which took place during the early years of his reign was based upon Portsmouth, and in the preparation of this he took great if not particularly intelligent interest. It was destined to sail, under his favourite, Lord High Admiral Buckingham, to La Rochelle, to help the Huguenots of France in their struggle against the French Crown; and his main preoccupation was to overcome the administrative chaos into which the country had fallen, and to get the fleet to sea as quickly as possible.

Charles himself failed as an administrator because he could never persuade his Parliaments (who held the purse-strings) to vote sufficient money to the naval service. So, although he succeeded in producing a few ships (and some, like the *Sovereign*, much larger and more extravagantly adorned than was necessary) by using doubtfully legal devices like Ship Money, he could not equip them as they should have been equipped, or man them as they should have been manned. But this was not through lack of trying, still less through lack of enthusiasm. He was mad-keen to get them provisioned, gunned, ammunitioned, and in all ways properly set up. So, as the ships lay at Spithead, he decided to hurry them on by coming down to Portsmouth in person, not to review them – that would in the circumstances be a waste of time and money – but to visit all the principal vessels separately, view their state of readiness (or absence of it) and get to know their commanding officers and their people. When he arrived, it was already June 11 (1627) – full late in the year to start on a campaign, and the fleet was supposed to be ready. It was not; but at least it was as nearly ready as it was ever likely to be. Characteristically, too, he brought down from Town with him a large retinue of gilded but idle nobility and gentry who could hardly have furthered the real preparations.

Still, he arrived and began his visitation early in the morning. The first ship which he reached was the *Victory*, lying in the harbour mouth. Thence, after due civilities exchanged with the officers on board, and after a careful examination of guns, ropes and stores, he was carried on to the *Rainbow*, where the same performance took place. Then he came to the *Triumph* – and now it was time for dinner.

That meal, what with all the hangers-on, proved rather lengthy and one gets the distinct impression that a good time was had by all, for 'dinner passed away with as much mirth as Sir Robert Deall, the Fool Archie, and the Duke's musicians could make'.[1] The jollities, however, finally came to an end, and 'after dinner, he went on board the *Warspite*, the *Repulse* and the *Vanguard*, and thence ashore', landing in Stokes Bay and going off to view the fortifications. Certainly the King meant well, and his naval servants may have derived some benefit from his presence, but how much we shall probably never know. It is not clear, however, in what respect they could have done worse than they did, for a greater fiasco than this Isle de Rhé expedition has never disgraced our naval annals before or since.

The later days of Charles I, as all know, were tragic. Moreover, the King, in losing the Civil War, lost (as well as his life) all his property, including his personal possession of the ships of his Navy. These, under the Commonwealth, became first the Parliament's ships, but then, after the Restoration, the People's ships: not Charles II's ships, though – clever fellow as he was – it was he

[1] Cal. State Papers Dom., June 11, 1627.

157

who first called them the 'Royal Navy', pretending that they were still his. This is somehow characteristic of the topsy-turvy way we Englishmen approach things. Here was the very first king who did not own the ships, conferring on them – for the first time – the epithet which surely implies Kingly ownership.

Still, even if he did not own them, he undoubtedly loved them, as he loved everything to do with the sea. And, unlike his predecessors, he was not content to be taken in boats to see his beloved ships. He went, whenever he felt like it, to look at them from the deck of his own yacht. He was the first of our monarchs to possess such a luxury, and the first to take up sailing as a sport. In his time he owned a whole succession of yachts. The Dutch gave him his first at his restoration. It was called the *Mary*. The following year he had another called the *Katherine* – and so, incidentally, had his brother, James Duke of York, who was just as keen (his was called the *Anne*). They were all about 100 tons burden, and the royal brothers constantly raced with each other. The names of some of these yachts became almost endemic, and lasted throughout the eighteenth century. But in his own lifetime, like a really enthusiastic racing yachtsman, he was always changing his boats. He had a whole fleet of them. During his reign and that of his brother, no less than twenty-six were built.

Though he was at Portsmouth among his ships certainly in 1661, if not in the very year of his restoration, he did not have the opportunity of inspecting them in bulk until he went down in 1665, as the fleet was mobilizing for the Second Dutch War. But as, this time, he travelled by road, it is doubtful whether he actually *reviewed* the array. Probably – like his father some thirty-eight years before – he *visited* them. Yet such a visit would be an altogether more professional affair than Charles I's, because he really knew what to look for on board. And when the fleet returned to Spithead after its first battle – off Lowestoft – there was Charles again to inspect it.

And as his never-wavering interest continued, one feels that whenever Charles grew weary of the intrigues and the scandals of Whitehall, he came away – sometimes almost slunk away – either by road or by sea to Portsmouth and Spithead. When the Third

Dutch War was brewing, in the summer of 1671, he was there again to view the fleet as it assembled. And this time he even went to sea with it and was caught in the easterly gale which greeted it as it emerged from St Helens and dispersed it. So he landed in Devonshire and came home by road.

On May 3 in the following year, when the war was really about to begin, and a squadron of those unaccustomed allies, the French, had arrived to join our forces at Spithead, here was a naval occasion which he could not bear to miss. So once more he was at Portsmouth, this time to inspect, and actually to review, the combined Anglo-French fleet, now under the command of his brother, the Duke of York. At this review, we learn, there were nearly 100 ships, 24,000 men and 6,000 guns. There were great hopes of a famous victory; but it did not materialize. The hostile fleets met off Solebay, and the French squadron managed to sail in one direction while the two English squadrons went off in another. The great Dutch Admiral De Ruyter made the most of this accident and succeeded in setting on fire the *Royal James*, one of our newest ships and now the flagship of Pepys's patron, the Earl of Sandwich. The Earl, his ship ablaze, had to transfer his flag to another ship, but during the transfer the small boat overturned and his Lordship, who was enormously fat, burdened with armour and unable to swim, drowned. Otherwise the encounter ended approximately all-square. And just after the war was over, Charles went to Spithead once again, accompanied by Samuel Pepys, to pay a visit to Sir John Narbrough's flagship.

The Dutch Wars over, Charles was becoming increasingly entangled with his Parliament on the one hand and with Louis XIV of France on the other. So he had less occasion, as well as less time, to be down in Hampshire. Yet he was there once more – in June 1675 – when he came within a reasonable distance of being shipwrecked and drowned. This time he was bound for Portsmouth to witness the launching of a new *Royal James*, built to replace the one lost at Solebay. Again it was a naval occasion too dear for him to keep away from, and he went down to Spithead by sea in a small sixth-rate of only 180 tons called the *Greyhound*, but taking with him a whole squadron of yachts. Pepys, who had to be there too, arrived at Portsmouth on June 29, but there was no sign of the *Greyhound*, which should have arrived the day before. Then, on the 30th, the *Anne* yacht sailed in, carrying James Duke of York and a cargo of very bedraggled courtiers. As she had started from the Thames with the *Greyhound*, there was much anxiety for the King's sovereign safety, Pepys himself saying that only the King's well-known seamanship could save him – for that of the *Greyhound*'s Captain was, he said, no great shakes. Next day, however, their anxiety was relieved by the arrival of a runner from the outer side of the Isle of Wight, who brought news that the King had landed there, soaked to the skin, famished with hunger, but unbowed: and he reached Portsmouth on July 2.

Charles was delighted with the new *Royal James,* and he showed his appreciation by knighting its architect, Anthony Deane, as well as two of the Commissioners. Afterwards, at the earnest request of the courtiers, he re-embarked for the Thames in the far more adequate *Harwich*. It was during this trip that he saw two little yachts which Deane was building for Louis XIV, and fell in love with one of them – the *Cleveland* – of which he ordered a replica from Deane. There can be no doubt that he was as maritime-minded a monarch as has ever graced the throne of England – with the perhaps slightly ludicrous exception of William IV, the Sailor King.

When Charles died, to be succeeded by his brother James II, there was still a very navally-minded occupant of the throne: a man who had on two occasions commanded the English fleet in action with the Dutch; who had, for the first thirteen years of his brother's reign, been Lord High Admiral of England; who had as his right-hand man Mr Pepys himself; and who was as keen on sailing in swift boats as his brother. But King James II, who was always his own worst enemy, spent most of his short reign not healthily inspecting his ships at Spithead or anywhere else, but in alienating his subjects by trying to make them Roman Catholics against their inclination. But he knew Portsmouth well, for he had once been its governor and had there welcomed his brother's bride, Catherine of Braganza, on her arrival in England in 1662 (Plate 12). Once King himself, he did not altogether neglect the town. He was at least once down there, in 1687 when he inspected the fleet and fortifications of the town. His monogram, with this date upon it, still remains to commemorate the visit.

We have seen in another connection what a sorry mess he made of his reign, and how he finally lost the throne to his son-in-law, the Prince of Orange, who, as William III, began his joint reign with his wife, Queen Mary II, in 1689. William was a great statesman as well as an experienced if not quite a great soldier, and so he always recognized the importance of the English Navy, and always wished it well – though perhaps he was rather keener on his Army. But by nature he was a sad and rather a soured man, without any of King Charles II's natural charm, and he never lost his thick Dutch accent. But, as ruler of both England and Holland, he had much shuttling to do between them, and he maintained a flotilla of eight yachts.

With his coming to the throne, England found herself at once plunged into war with France, William being, in fact, the head of all European opposition to the 'Sun King'. And, as early as April 1689, he sent the English Navy, under the unpleasant Admiral Herbert, to defend Ireland from a French fleet despatched by Louis to support James. The fleets met in Bantry Bay off the south-west corner of that country, and the action which followed was quite indecisive: indeed rather trivial. Thereupon Herbert returned straight away to Spithead whence he had recently come.

Now William, as we have said, was a statesman and, for all his rather rough manner, a diplomat too. He had not been occupying his throne for more than a few months, and, in the unusual state of English affairs, was not at all sure who was for him, and who was for James. He was not sure of the loyalty of all the fleet, or of the fleet commanders. So, when he heard that the Admiral had reached Spithead again, he hurried down to Portsmouth and boarded Herbert's flagship. Here he made himself as pleasant as he could to all the officers of the fleet from Herbert downwards, choosing to consider (though he must have known otherwise) that Bantry Bay had been a great and gallant victory for the Royal Navy in general and for Arthur Herbert in particular. For it was quite imperative, he knew, to keep the English fleet and everyone

in it as sweet as possible. Admiral Herbert was therefore created
Earl of Torrington on the spot; two of his leading officers, Captains
John Ashby and Cloudisley Shovell, were knighted; and a free gift of
ten shillings was distributed to every man on the Lower Deck.
He was at Portsmouth again in 1693, visiting the fleet to celebrate
a much more worthy victory. The twin battles of Barfleur and La
Hogue had been safely won: and he marked the occasion by going
on board Admiral Rooke's flagship and conferring on him the
honour of knighthood for his great share in the La Hogue victory.
After that, he spent most of his brief reign fighting on land – in
Ireland and in the Low Countries – so that he had no time for
Spithead and the ships there, though he fitted them cleverly
enough into his scheme of strategy.

It was a long time before the crown of England (or, after 1707,
of Great Britain) began to have intimate relations again with the
Navy. Queen Anne's connection with it was never very close,
though for a time (in 1708) she was actually Lord High Admiral,
while her husband, Prince George of Denmark, occupied that high
office from 1702 to 1708. He, however, was not a man who could
make any office exciting, being by reputation the dullest man who
ever lived.[1]

Anne's successor, George I, did not exactly sparkle either. He
could not speak English, and was anyway not interested in the
Royal Navy, or in anything much beyond his beloved Hanover.
But, like William, he had a great deal of shuttling to do – now
between England and Hanover – and he possessed a fleet of no
less than fifteen yachts. Nor was his son 'Dettingen' George II
much better, being no English-speaker but in most ways a
foreigner. Neither of these monarchs paid much attention to the
Senior Service which during their reigns was markedly neglected,
especially during the premiership of Sir Robert Walpole, who had
no use for the Navy at all. Nor, so far as we know, did either of the
first two Georges ever put in an appearance at Spithead, though it

[1] Charles II nicknamed him 'Est-il possible?' because that was his
invariable answer to any remark addressed to him; and Charles's verdict
on him is well known – 'I have tried him drunk, and I have tried him
sober. But, drunk or sober, there is nothing to him.'

was the base from which Commodore Anson sailed for his famous voyage round the world, and the port to which he returned. His victory of the first Battle of Finisterre also was won from here.

It is hardly necessary to say that George II never came anywhere near Portsmouth during the disgraceful events which led up to the judicial murder of Admiral Byng (see p. 107). Nor, during the last year of his life, did he notice his fleets as they sailed from and returned to Spithead in the course of that 'Wonderful Year' of 1759. He did not see Admiral Saunders and General Wolfe set out from here for America in February, nor was he there to welcome in November the dead body of this servant who had captured Quebec and Canada for him.

But things began to change when his young grandson, George III, came to the throne in 1760: an ambitious (probably over-ambitious) lad who set great store by his Englishry. During his long reign he made a point of visiting Portsmouth and Spithead whenever he had a reasonable excuse. His first visit took place in June 1773 and he stayed for four days inspecting the veterans of the Seven Years' War fleet at Spithead and distributing largesse both there and in the dockyard. It is this Royal Visit that, to this day, the Admiralty regards as being the 'First Review', all later ones following it being in the tradition then set up. It is not clear why the authorities have disregarded the pageants of Henry VIII and Charles II. Perhaps they do not regard those earlier ones as being formal enough, or, more likely, they have clean forgotten the existence of the sixteenth- and seventeenth-century junketings which never became common enough to grow into traditions. But the visit of 1773 constituted a full-dress Review, the King actually making a tour of the fleet in his barge (Plate 13).

He came again in May 1778, bringing his Queen with him, when to honour him the people of the town wore laurels and blue ribbons in their hats. This time he inspected a new dock. War with France broke out again immediately afterwards, and though activities at Spithead went on unabated, there was perhaps nothing much of glory which he could seize upon to celebrate – there was no particular credit in the manœuvres of Sir Charles Hardy in 1779 (see p. 77), nor in the lamentable tragedy of the *Royal George* in 1782 (see p. 86). But when the War of the French Revolution began in 1793 and the pattern of naval achievement began to improve, he soon found opportunities. In 1794 Lord Howe won the battle instantly dubbed 'The Glorious First of June' and, though it turned out on second thoughts to be not all that glorious, it was, in George's opinion and the Government's, an event well worth celebrating.

Howe's fleet returned to Spithead with its six French prizes on June 15, and on the 25th the King came down, bringing his Queen again and several of his children as well as some of his chief ministers. Sir William Dillon, then a Midshipman, describes[1] the visit and the King's awards.

They went on board the *Queen Charlotte*. To the noble and gallant Admiral Lord Howe, His Majesty presented a diamond-hilted sword of the value of 3,000 guineas: also a gold chain to be worn round the neck. The Royal Party dined that day on board with his Lordship. It was whispered on that occasion that the King intended investing the peer with the Order of the Garter... However, rumours in circulation led me to believe that the ministers' political prejudices restrained the Royal will. After dinner the Royal party returned on shore. They were saluted and cheered by the whole Fleet, both coming and going.

The two next senior Admirals, Graves and Hood, were created Irish peers: the four Rear-Admirals, baronets. All the Flag Officers received gold chains similar to that given to Lord Howe, and the Captains received medals – at least, a certain number of them.[2] Pensions were settled on all that were wounded. All the Senior Lieutenants of the ships of the line that were in action received the rank of Commander. The Master of the *Queen Charlotte*, Mr Bowen, was made a Lieutenant;

---

[1] *Dillon's Narrative* (Navy Records Society, 1953), vol. i, p. 150.

[2] There were some strange omissions – the strangest Captain Collingwood who, however, received one later. These medals were the first of all naval medals, and when the Naval General Service Medal was issued in 1848, not only did it date back to the first of June, 1794, but also the ribbon chosen was the same white and blue-edged one.

and later, became a Commissioner and a Rear-Admiral – a rare feat in those days for a mere Warrant Officer.

After this, His Majesty remained for several days, holding a series of levées, and doing all he could to enhance the Navy's reputation. But he did not hold a formal Review, leading the fleet in his own yacht. In fact, he probably did not possess a yacht at that time or, at any rate, did not have it with him at Portsmouth.

Early in the next century George III unfortunately became insane and so could not continue to visit his fleet at Spithead. His place, however, was taken by the Prince Regent who, both before he came to the throne as George IV and after it, showed the greatest interest in the anchorage and the ships moored there. He had his own yacht, and often cruised in it on the Solent, sometimes to the embarrassment of their Lordships, who found the resulting ceremonies a waste of the ships' time. He paid his first official visit in August 1803 and, after cruising round on his own for some three weeks, returned for a full-scale review and inspection on September 14.

Thereafter the exigencies of the Napoleonic War rather cramped his style. For the ships were much too hard-pressed to have time for such frivolities as reviews. There was, however, one political occasion in 1812, when the Comte de Lille, who hoped soon to become Louis XVIII of France, paid an official visit to Spithead. All the big-wigs of Great Britain were there to greet him – for, after all, it was our duty to welcome the representative of the *ancien régime,* just as it was our duty to down in every possible way the Corsican usurper. The Count, we learn, took his breakfast with Captain Graham Moore in the *Chatham,* and was then conducted on a sight-seeing cruise right round the Isle of Wight.

After that the Regent had to wait patiently until 1819 when, peace restored, he passed the whole of August cruising and lazing about Spithead and the Solent in his Royal Yacht. And now Dillon, risen to the rank of a senior Captain, met him again, and, being something of a tuft-hunter, positively basked in the attentions which the Prince paid him. And during all this time, though neither inspecting nor reviewing the fleet officially, he was

165

interfering with routine by his numerous visits to various ships and
the various Admirals' numerous visits to his yacht.

In the following year, in September, he returned in triumph as
King, when he held an official inspection. But it was not very long
after this that he began to grow extremely wayward and unpre-
dictable, inclining more and more to shut himself off from the
world.

It was now his brother's turn. The 'Sailor Prince' had, of course,
been a serving naval officer in his younger days, and a very keen
one too, if an over-hard disciplinarian. He too – when the Admiralty no longer employed him – liked nothing better than to hang
around Spithead. In 1818, for instance, he went there, embarked
in the *Spartan*, and went to sea in her.

In 1827 he was – rather surprisingly – made Lord High Admiral,
an office which had been in abeyance for over a century. One of the
first things he did was to bring a squadron round to Spithead and
to hold an inspection of all the ships anchored there. It was on
this occasion that his ship had the novel experience of being taken
in tow by one of the first steamships, the *Lightning*, which – against
the wind – 'brought her into the harbour in a beautiful manner
amidst the cheers of thousands of most respectable people
assembled on the lines and beaches' (plate 14). Thereafter he
stayed for ten days, which enabled him, on August 8, also to
inspect a Russian squadron of nine sail of the line, eight large
frigates and a corvette which had conveniently made its appearance
in Spithead.

Only three months later he was there again, once more inspecting the fleet, but especially the *Galatea* and the Experimental
Squadron which at that time was deeply engaging the Admiralty's
attention. And, not content with this, he came back a third time
after another three months, this time to inspect Admiral Codring-
ton's fleet which had just returned victorious from fighting the
Battle of Navarino. After that, the Government persuaded him
to relinquish the Lord High Admiralship in some haste, but not
before he had succeeded in altering all the white facings of officers'
uniforms into red ones. When he came to the throne in 1830 his
eccentricities increased more and more. He often frequented

ROYAL YACHTS, VISITS AND REVIEWS

Portsmouth and Spithead but, oddly enough, as King of England
he was more easily kept in control than he had been as Lord High
Admiral. For by then the monarchy had become a very limited
monarchy indeed, as well as a very unpopular one.

With the accession of Queen Victoria, Fleet Reviews became,
for almost the first time, regular institutions and almost features of
national policy. Previous sovereigns had fairly often inspected
the fleets (whether qualified to do so or not), but, it was felt, the
Queen, being a lady, was not so qualified – indeed, she felt it herself.
Yet, like most of her predecessors, she was acutely conscious of
the Navy's importance and was greatly attached to many of the
senior officers of her day. There is no doubt, in fact, that she liked
the company of her ships and the entertaining of her officers in
the Royal Yacht. There were as well two other reasons why the
Naval Review figured so prominently in the scheme of things in her
day. It was, first, a very good way of showing other countries the
might of Great Britain, and how rash it would be to challenge that
might. For it could all be done in such a seemly way, and all under
the guise of polite entertainment. What more delightful, more
civilized, than to invite foreign potentates for a cruise in one's
yacht, and what more natural, while they were on board, than to
take them round the fleet?

There was also another motive behind the authorities' insistence
upon Reviews. We have reached the days when the power of the
press was becoming greater and greater; and not only the press,
but also, with the ever-enlarging franchise, there were now far
more people whose views on things had to be considered: the
people who now had votes, the people who paid the taxes. And to
the authorities a touch of pageantry seemed to be an admirable
thing. 'Let as many taxpayers as possible see for themselves how
we are spending their money. Let them see what good and reliable
people they have chosen to govern them. Let them see for themselves how capable their Navy is of defending them against
envious outsiders!'

The Queen's long reign covered nearly the whole period of the
great transition of ships from wood to iron and then to steel; the
transition of motive power from sail to steam; and the transition

of broadside, smooth-bored roundshot-firing guns to leviathans of breech-loading, rifled, shell-firers. This gives great interest to all the different reviews; though we must not here get too deeply involved in the kaleidoscopic changes which were taking place.

The first review of her reign took place in June 1845, when the Queen went round the fleet at Spithead in the Royal Yacht *Victoria and Albert I,* when she also witnessed the departure on a cruise of the Experimental Squadron.

The first really important Review, however, was that held at Spithead on the outbreak of the Crimean War in 1854. At that moment very nearly all the great ships were still, as it were, 'improved *Victories*' – wooden, with sail-power only and with long rows of broadside solid-shotted guns. The fleet under Admiral Sir Charles Napier was fitted out at Portsmouth, and the Queen came down to see it off, accompanying it for some way in her yacht, the *Fairy.* The other half of our ships, destined for the Black Sea, were fitted out in the Mediterranean, and so could not set out with Her Majesty's blessing. Neither half of the fleet in fact distinguished itself greatly. But in 1856, when the war was over, no less than 254 ships gathered at Spithead to be reviewed again (Plate 15). As a result of experience gained during the war, the fleet now took on a very mixed appearance. A few even of the biggest ships were screw-propelled (though strictly sail-propelled too), but among the smaller craft there were many which now relied for their motion upon either screw or paddle. There were even three little ships which had just joined the fleet and (like the French gunboats used at the bombardment of Kinburn) were cased in armour. These were the very first armoured ships in the Royal Navy. None of the bigger vessels carried it at all.

As soon as the war was over, the Queen, the whole of the Royal Family, the whole Board of Admiralty and the Commanders-in-Chief of the Black Sea and the Baltic fleets embarked on the new Royal Yacht *Victoria and Albert II* and spent a long day at Spithead. The fleet was anchored in two lines. It then weighed anchor in succession and passed the yacht, making a sham attack on Southsea Castle. *The Times* waxed lyrical about it all. This magnificent review of 250 stern vessels of war, it said, might be considered as the inauguration of a new era in naval science. This was not the view of the experts, nor of posterity. Most of the ships were already out of date and would probably have given a very poor account of themselves had they been called upon to fight.

In 1867 the Sultan of Turkey paid a visit to the Queen, and a Review in his honour was held. This time the fleet was divided into two separate squadrons, a wooden one and an ironclad one. In the iron portion there were twelve battleships, the most famous of which was the *Warrior*, a steamer built of iron with $4\frac{1}{2}$-inch-thick armour on her sides, but still carrying smooth-bore broadside guns. She was capable of doing 14·4 knots under steam, but carried a full set of masts and yards for sailing. One ship only – the *Bellerophon* – had her guns mounted in a central battery. The wooden squadron consisted of a wonderful hotch-potch of new and old – mostly old. This time, only seventy-four ships were present, but in power they would probably have seen off easily the 250 at the previous Review.

Six years later the Shah of Persia turned up, and the fleet was again reviewed. Once more there was a very mixed bag of ships. Even among the best of them, the twenty-three largest could be classed into twelve distinct groups. Incidentally, with no battle experience behind any of them, no one had any idea how they would behave in action. A ship – and an interesting one – that should have graced this Review was the ill-fated *Captain*. She had been built to the specification not of the professional naval architects, but of that brilliant amateur Captain Cowper Coles. She incorporated all his pet ideas. She carried her guns in turrets (like the American *Monitor*) but she was a full-rigged ship carrying an enormous spread of canvas. Great things were expected of her. But unfortunately she had a very low freeboard and, when under full sail, proved monstrously top-heavy: so much so that, when out off the coast of Spain on her trial run, she suddenly turned turtle in not too bad a gale, drowning all but eighteen of her crew of 490. She only just misses, in fact, her place in our 'Accidents' chapter, because she had sailed from Spithead for her trials and to Spithead she was due to return.

There was a big Review in 1886 on the occasion of the Colonial and Indian Exhibition. But that of July 1887 was an even bigger one. It marked the Queen's Golden Jubilee. Things were beginning to straighten themselves out. All the big ships were now of iron, and armoured: armoured indeed immensely thickly. The biggest – though not the newest – ship among them was the *Inflexible*, of all but 12,000 tons and carrying on her sides iron armour which was no less than 24 inches thick. There was also an armoured cruiser of 8,400 tons called the *Impérieuse*, and there were numerous torpedo-boats, for a rather ineffectual torpedo had arrived in the seventies and been greatly improved in the eighties.

Ten years later came the Diamond Jubilee Review. Now there were whole classes of all-but identical steel battleships displacing 14,900 tons, and muzzle-loaders had at last given way to breech-loaders. All the old types had disappeared into the limbo where old ironmongery goes: the Motherbank must have been heavily populated in the nineties. But it was not these monsters which stole the limelight this time. All eyes were fixed instead upon a tiny but pioneer vessel, the *Turbinia*. Built privately by the Hon. Charles Parsons, she was the world's first turbine-propelled ship, capable of the then incredible speed of $34\frac{1}{2}$ knots (Plate 16). She trespassed into the stately ranks of naval ships, and to the fury of the brass hats even the fastest destroyers failed lamentably to intercept the intruder. But the hint was taken, and the *Turbinia* episode marked the beginning of a great revolution in warship engines.

There was another ship, too, which should have been present at Spithead on that day in 1897. The *Victoria*, of 10,475 tons, was in 1893 the flagship of the Mediterranean fleet carrying the flag of Vice-Admiral Sir George Tryon. On manœuvres off Beirut, the fleet was sailing in two columns of line ahead, 1,200 yards apart. Tryon now proposed to invert the line, the leading ships – the *Victoria* and the *Camperdown* – to do so by turning towards each other. Obviously all depended upon the diameter of the turning circle of each ship, and almost everyone on board soon realized with dismay that whereas the turning circle of the *Victoria* was 600 yards, that of the *Camperdown* was distinctly greater. Everybody saw it but, apparently, no one dared to say anything, for George Tryon was well known for being a bit of a tartar. So the inevitable happened, and at a speed of 5 or 6 knots the murderous ram of the *Camperdown* crashed into the side of the *Victoria*, ripping out a hole well under the water line of 28 feet high by 12 feet broad. For a while they remained locked together, but as soon as the *Camperdown* backed out, the *Victoria* went down like a stone. Tryon could probably have been saved, but presumably he did not want to live under the circumstances, and was among the 358 officers and men who were lost. Another officer who went down in the *Victoria* but who mercifully for Britain was rescued, was none other than her commander, John Rushworth Jellicoe.

The fleet in the 1897 Review was drawn up in four columns, and there was a fifth reserved for foreign men-of-war representing other navies. The British contingent was 21 battleships, 37 cruisers and many smaller craft – 165 ships in all. Submarines had not quite appeared, though they were only just round the corner. Nor were seaplanes, or indeed any aircraft, in existence – it was only in 1903 that the first heavier-than-air machine left the ground.

In January 1901 Victoria died at Osborne on the Isle of Wight, and her body had to be taken to Windsor for burial. When that day arrived, the whole of the Channel and the Reserve fleets were moored in one line from Cowes to Spithead. It was just like a farewell Review as the old Queen steamed slowly past them in H.M.Y. *Alberta,* accompanied by her family, including her son-in-law, Kaiser Wilhelm II.

The new King's Coronation Review (delayed by his illness) took place at Spithead on August 16, 1902. The squadron of Royal Yachts, led by the Trinity House yacht *Irene,* was now four in number, the principal one (which carried the King) being the new *Victoria and Albert III.* In 1905, to celebrate the *Entente Cordiale,* the French fleet came to Spithead to visit the British fleet, and the King reviewed both from the Royal Yacht.

But now, as we turn the century, comes 'Jacky' Fisher, the creator of the really modern Royal Navy, with his all-big-gun battleships, the Dreadnoughts, and the great naval arms race with the Kaiser's Germany. By the time of Edward VII's death in May

1910 the race was on, and the fleet had already increased considerably in size when the new King reviewed it in the summer of 1911. But it was in July 1914 that the greatest naval pageant of all time happened – in sheer numbers of ships, at any rate. But this was not, technically, just another Review. It was something altogether more serious, a full-scale test mobilization, with the whole of the naval reserves called out. It took the outward form of a Review, however, and King George V in the Royal Yacht sailed for endless miles up and down through the long sea-lanes of sombre grey-painted warships of all kinds. The impact upon all those who witnessed it was enough to last a lifetime. And amongst others, the present writer, then a young man on the staff of the Royal Naval College, Osborne, was privileged to view the whole unique sight from the top of a turret in the Dreadnought *Centurion*. He has never forgotten it: the spectacle of the greatest Navy which had ever existed, drawn up all ready to do battle in what was soon to be the greatest of all wars ever to be fought to date. Moreover, the test mobilization turned out to have been superbly timed, if accidentally so. For that great fleet was not demobilized again when its original period was up. Instead, it sailed straight off to take up its fore-ordained battle stations for the First World War.

Naturally the whole might of the Royal Navy was not assembled at Spithead on that summer's day. There were a few ships, of cruiser size and smaller, that were widely flung over the seas of the earth in their normal peace-time stations, and there were present only a fraction of the fleets of the British Dominions so soon to join the Royal Navy in the fight. But, so that the reader may form some idea of the size of that great gathering, it is worth recording the full strength of the British Navy at the outbreak of war. And then, if we see what the figures were at the end of it, we shall get some idea of the resilience of the Royal Navy.

| *Warships* | August 4, 1914 | | November 11, 1918 | |
| --- | --- | --- | --- | --- |
| Battleships | | | | |
| Dreadnoughts | 20 | | 33 | |
| Pre-Dreadnoughts | 40 | 60 | 17 | 50 |
| Battle Cruisers | | 9 | | 9 |
| Cruisers | | 46 | | 27 |
| Light Cruisers | | 62 | | 82 |
| Gunboats | | 28 | | 52 |
| Sloops | | 11 | | 11 |
| Monitors | | – | | 33 |
| Coast Defence Vessel | | – | | 1 |
| Fleet sweeping Vessels (sloops) | | – | | 106 |
| Flotilla Leaders | | 1 | | 26 |
| Torpedo Boat Destroyers | | 215 | | 407 |
| Torpedo Boats | | 106 | | 94 |
| Submarines | | 76 | | 137 |
| Aircraft Carriers | | 1 | | 13 |
| Minelayers | | 7 | | 8 |
| P. & P.C. Boats | | – | | 62 |
| Repair Ships | | 2 | | 7 |
| Depot Ships | | 22 | | 49 |
| Miscellaneous | | 2 | | 15 |
| Armed Merchant Cruisers | | – | | 29 |
| Armed Boarding Steamers | | – | | 20 |
| Special Service Ships | | – | | 50 |
| Coastal Motor Boats | | – | | 66 |
| Total Warships | | 648 | | 1,354 |

| Auxiliary Patrol Service | August 4, 1914 | November 11, 1918 |
|---|---|---|
| Trawlers | 12 | 1,520 |
| Yachts | – | 57 |
| Patrol Gunboats | – | 30 |
| Whalers | – | 18 |
| Drifters | – | 1,365 |
| Minesweepers | – | 156 |
| Motor Launches | – | 507 |
| Motor Drifters and Boats | – | 74 |
| Total Auxiliary Patrol Service | 12 | 3,727 |
| *Grand Total* | 660 | 5,081 |

By November 1918 the fleet was fined down and tailored to modern war. The lessons that we learned, especially from the German U-boats, all tended to fewer big ships but a multitude of much smaller ones, to hunt the near-invincible foe. At the end, the fleet was not so spectacular to look at, had less majesty, but it was something like eight times as large in sheer numbers.

There was no big Review at Spithead at the end of the war, but King George V – in his younger days a professional sailor – certainly never neglected it, going out with the fleet on its practices and even, more than once, reviewing it – but at Weymouth, not Spithead. As the inter-war years went on, the world came – pathetically – to rely more and more upon the League of Nations; and in the thirties something very like a wave of pacifism swept the country. So until Hitler arose in Nazi Germany and began rattling the sabre in the middle thirties, the Navy had a very thin time of it. It was all rather like the days of Walpole repeating themselves after 200 years. Between 1918 and 1936, for instance, we only laid down two capital ships, the *Nelson* and the *Rodney*, and even they proved to be none of the best. Fortunately for us, however, in and after 1936 the German Führer became so very blatant in his quest for the hegemony of the world that we had some time in which to put our house in order. In that year five super-Dreadnoughts and six large aircraft carriers were laid down. They were not ready when war broke out in September 1939, but they were well on the way and began to join the fleet in 1940.

But again it was not in battleships that we needed reinforcement. The surface fleet of Germany in 1939 did not compare with that of the Kaiser in 1914. Again it was the U-boat which became our principal enemy – the U-boat allied now with air power. And again, as the war progressed, we found that our fleet was the wrong shape. In the course of it, in fact, that age-old war-winner, the battleship, went right out of the picture, to be replaced by the aircraft carrier, the aeroplane and hosts of small anti-submarine craft.

The war started in 1939 quite differently from 1914. There was nothing like the Test Mobilization of that year. Hitler had made his intentions so clear that we could with a perfectly good conscience start preparing almost from the beginning of the year. On May 29 the reservists began to be called up to man our extensive moth-ball fleet, and by August the Reserve Fleet was ready for the fray. It was inspected by King George VI but, as the ceremony took place in Weymouth Bay and not in Spithead, it is none of our business to describe it. He did not inspect the Active Service fleet, either at Spithead or anywhere, because it quietly went up to its war stations piecemeal, and was in position by the end of August.

In the five and three-quarter years of relentless war which followed, we suffered exceedingly heavy casualties at sea, both in ships and in men, especially in the Eastern Hemisphere where the U.S.A. and ourselves were suddenly attacked by the Japanese. In fact, in that part of the world we lost *all* our original naval forces though, before the end, we did succeed in securing again a naval presence in the Pacific and South East Asia. By 1945 we had replaced many of our losses. But that was hardly the trouble. What was the trouble was that everyone now knew that a revolution had taken place in the kind of naval forces that a nation required. And, of all our major units, really all except aircraft carriers were obsolete.

This was discouraging, coming at the time it did, when we were very war-weary and very impoverished: when in fact only the world-powers of the U.S.A. and the U.S.S.R. were in a position to take up all the running in naval armaments and in nuclear armaments too; and when the British Empire itself looked as if it must sink into at least the third place and cease to be one of the super-powers at all.

What has all this to do with Reviews? Well, it meant a great come-down from the Test Mobilization of 1914, when Spithead saw the greatest-ever assembly of fighting ships. The fact is that from 1945 onwards the British Navy had ceased to compete with the big battalions of America and Russia. In number, in size and in power we have really made no attempt to build up our naval might. And that – in terms of Naval Reviews – is distressing, to say the least of it. We still hold Reviews, and at Spithead too. But now they are – rather sadly, but rather markedly – different.

One was held in the summer of 1953 as a part of the ceremonies to mark the coronation of Queen Elizabeth II. That was quite soon after the end of the war, and most of the ships which had fought in that war were still extant, as well as one or two which, not being quite ready when hostilities ended, had been completed afterwards. The traditional ceremonies were religiously kept up. The Royal Yacht, with the Queen and the Duke of Edinburgh on board, was not yet the *Britannia*, but a naval sloop acting for it and called H.M.S. *Surprise*. She made her way round the fleet and at length cast her anchor at the head of the lines. The full suit of colours was flown, including the Royal Standard at the main. According to the best tradition too, the *Surprise* was led by the Trinity House yacht *Patricia* with the Elder Brethren on board, and followed by H.M.S. *Redpole*, also acting as a substitute for the Admiralty yacht, carrying all 'the Lords Commissioners for the execution of the Office of the Lord High Admiral' (Plate 17). There were one or two capital ships left, the showpiece being H.M.S. *Vanguard,* the most powerful battleship we ever possessed and destined to be the last we ever possessed. There were still a number of aircraft carriers which made a good show behind the *Vanguard*. There were also a number of representative ships from the fleets of our allies, including some from Russia. Otherwise there was not much that was impressive.

To approach as near as possible to today, it must be recorded that another Review was held in Spithead in the summer of 1969. The battleships had gone to the scrap-heap, but there was still a residue of British carriers – all under sentence of death but not yet dead.[1] So much for 'Majesty': but there were a number of powerful-looking and very modern vessels of about 10,000 tons, as well as a number of smaller ones and submarines, nuclear as well as conventional. And the whole display, one must admit, was quite striking to the view. But what made it striking? Well, not the fact that it was a Review of the British Navy. Strictly, it was not. It was a Review of the N.A.T.O. forces: only a percentage of all the ships present were entitled to fly the White Ensign. One must not exaggerate. The R.N. components of this N.A.T.O. fleet are in no sense despicable. They lack no doubt the majesty of the old days, but in the light of the new days they are exceedingly workmanlike; and – but for the paucity of their numbers as compared with those of the U.S.S.R. and the U.S.A. – they would without question give a good account of themselves if brought to action. Yet that 1969 Review did underline, as nothing else could, the failing strength of the Royal Navy. And what would King Harry have had to say about that? What Charles Stuart? What even old Farmer George?

Is it one of the vagaries of history that, in the very year of this latest Review at Spithead, there should have appeared, for the very first time in that anchorage's long history, an Admiral who bears its name, and who is to be known as Flag Officer, Spithead?

[1] And sentence of death for one has lately been postponed.

# Chapter VIII

# LEVELS

A. *Under Spithead*

All in all, Spithead has not played a very prominent part in the development of the submarine. The reason for this is the estuarial nature of her waters. Submarines, and particularly modern ones, require deeper water than exists in the Solent for their operation and even for practising in. They can, and they do, use Portsmouth Harbour, coming in and leaving it on the surface. They have a depot at H.M.S. *Dolphin* in Haslar Creek and they have been a feature of every naval Review of this century – ever since, in fact, in their infancy in 1903, 'Jacky' Fisher had enthusiastically attended the exercises of the first flotilla of them to be formed in the Channel beyond St Helens. They can also of course on occasions operate successfully in confined waters, as the German U-boat commander, Lieutenant Prien, taught us to our chagrin in the autumn of 1939 when, with great skill and daring, he penetrated the defences of Scapa Flow and sank the battleship *Royal Oak* lying at anchor there. But still, when all is said, Spithead never is, and never has been, a happy hunting-ground for submarines.

But there are other fish – and mammals too – besides submarines that cruise from time to time beneath the surface of Spithead. On January 14 1819, for instance, an enormous porpoise was taken in St Helens Roads. It was eleven feet long all but an inch, and its girth was six feet; it weighed between ten and eleven hundredweight, and it had eighty-four awesome teeth. Some years later, in October 1823, an even larger visitor crossed Spithead and blundered into the Harbour. It was a beaked whale.

> On Thursday, just before the thunderstorm which happened on that afternoon, it went up Haslar-lake, where, on the ebb of the tide, it was left in a hole excavated for laying up the Rev. C. North's yacht, and was shortly afterwards discovered by some of the villagers of Alverstoke, who killed it and secured the carcass. It was twenty-four feet in length and upwards of twelve feet in circumference, and it required five horses to draw it on shore.[1]

It was, in fact, not all that much smaller than one of the earlier submarines.

B. *On the Surface of Spithead*

From the earliest times, in order to reach the great ships lying at the anchorage, or to pass to and from the Isle of Wight, men had used sailing vessels or rowed craft for the purpose. But early in the nineteenth century steamers began to appear. We have seen the 'Sailor King' being towed triumphantly back to Portsmouth by H.M.S. *Lightning* in 1827. But this was not by any means the first appearance of steam at the anchorage. In 1812 one Henry Bell, a Clydeside hotel proprietor, had launched on that river, for pleasure and for plain travel, a little ship he called the *Comet*. This was such a success with the Scots that the English in their turn demanded a similar pleasure. In 1815, therefore, another of the early Clyde steamers, the *Duke of Argyll*, was bought by a London firm, and after converting her into a sea-going boat and changing her name to *Thames*, they sent her forth on the long passage from Greenock to London. She passed down the Irish Sea and rounded Cornwall. Here the conservative natives, never having seen such a thing before, thought she was on fire and made a gallant attempt to put her out. Then she steamed up the Sound to Plymouth, and then, still attracting wide-spread comment (some of it pretty rude), she came at length to Spithead, which

[1] John Slight, *A History of Portsmouth* (1828), p. 243.

179

she crossed, her great paddles churning up the unaccustomed waters, and entered Portsmouth Harbour. She was the very first steamer to come that way, and such was the excitement that a court martial in progress in the guardship was rudely interrupted as the Admiral and all rushed on deck to view the phenomenon, the foretaste of the future. After detailed inspection by the authorities the next morning, the steamer went on her way to give the Londoners their treat. She did some service on the Thames, and later returned to Spithead to join a new ferry service just starting to ply between Portsmouth and Ryde.

It was not until 1821 that the Admiralty – rather shamefacedly – bought a second-hand steamer into its service to use as a tug. Its name, almost forgotten now, was the *Monkey*, and for some years it clanked and wheezed between the harbour mouth and Spithead and back again. As it was able to tow against the wind, it proved so time-saving that, after a while, their Lordships built a steam-tug of their very own which they called (like Bell's early Clydeside effort) the *Comet*. That they were just a little ashamed of such ugly, grimy and smelly craft is revealed by the fact that they refused to allow any of them to figure in the august pages of their official Navy List. The first steamer to be mentioned there was our friend the *Lightning* of 1827.

It was two years before this that, for the first time, the public were able to cross the Solent propelled by something other than sail or oar. On April 8, 1825 the first vessel of the Union Steam Packet picked up its passengers from the town and landed them at Ryde. It would seem that this new service put out of joint the noses of some of the Isle of Wight watermen. Anyway, the new company, probably by way of compensation, distributed to them, gratis, on that first day, two hogsheads of beer; and perhaps the watermen of Portsmouth were feeling the breeze too, because two hogsheads also went to them. Thereafter, paddle steamers quickly established themselves on the regular ferry routes to the Island.

c. *Just Above Spithead*

Steamer has remained the normal way of visiting the Island. But in July 1965, another and very popular sort of ferry was

introduced: the hovercraft (Plate 18). It was indeed on this Spithead crossing that the first hovercraft ferry service in the world
began. To this age of ours speed is very dear, and now it takes
only a minimum of seven minutes to make the crossing from
Portsmouth to Ryde, and twenty minutes from Portsmouth to
Cowes. In the old days of sail, it *might* have been done on a fresh
following wind in an hour, or even a little less. But it might have
taken three or four times as long, and it might not have been possible to do it at all.

Nowadays there are three services: one, run by Hovercraft
Travel Ltd, starts from a jetty beside the Clarence Pier, Southsea,
and ends at another jetty beside Ryde Pier. This service was
inaugurated in July 1965, and it takes seven minutes to cover the
distance. The second, run by British Railways, starts from the
Portsmouth Harbour terminus and ends at Ryde Pier head. The
service began in August 1968, and takes ten minutes on the passage,
which is rather longer than the Clarence Pier one. The third
(also run by British Railways) crosses from Portsmouth Harbour
to Cowes and takes twenty minutes.

D. *High Over Spithead*

On March 29, 1784, the crews of His Majesty's ships lying at
Spithead must have seen a sight which made them blink. They
saw – doubtless for the first time – fellow human beings riding high
up in the air. For on that day Portsmouth's first balloon was sent
up from Sadler's Wells, a cheap rival to the town's official theatre.
Behind the ascent, but probably not on it, was a local character
named Luke Kent, a well-known figure in the Portsmouth of his
day. But presumably the fleet got only an indifferent view of the
balloonists. Where they landed we are not told. But it was no
doubt somewhere on the mainland. Safety would seem to demand
that a southerly wind be blowing, so that the balloon would not
drift over the ships, but in a northerly direction.

It is not intended, however, to follow the general story of
aeronautics over Spithead. One particular phase of them only will
engage our attention here, and that is the competition for the
Schneider Marine Trophy. This event – perhaps one should not

say sporting event, though to the credit of all concerned it certainly was that – fluttered the dovecotes of all Western Europe and the U.S.A. between the years 1913 and 1931, and its great climax in the last-named year was essentially a chapter in the history of Spithead.

Jacques Schneider, a well-known French engineer and sportsman, presented the trophy (valued at 25,000 francs) in 1913, to be awarded every year to the pilot of the plane which completed a set course in the shortest time. Originally in the nature of a race between individuals, the competition after a time took on a strong national flavour, and ultimately became a trial of strength between the world powers, with teams of three flying officers entered from each state. The rules were very fair. The flights were to take place entirely over the sea, because the types entered had to be sea-planes or flying boats. This in the early days was a precautionary measure, since in 1913 all flying was very much in its infancy, and accidents over the sea were less likely to be fatal than over the land. Schneider being a Frenchman, the first contest was to be held off the coast of France: but after that the winner's country was to be the venue for the next race. The length of the course was to be 350 kilometres, or 217·49 miles. And lastly, any country which won the race three times out of five consecutive contests was to keep the Trophy in perpetuity.

The first race, then, was held off Monaco, and was won by a French pilot at an average speed of 45·75 m.p.h. If that speed seems trivial to us, let us recall that only ten years had passed since the first aeroplane had flown. The 1914 contest, again at Monaco, was won by an Englishman, C. Howard Pixton, in a Sopwith Seaplane at 86·8 m.p.h. At this point the First World War interrupted the series, and the next event, in 1919, due to be held off Bournemouth, had to be abandoned because of fog. The English sportingly waived their claim to holding the 1920 race in favour of the Italians who, in 1919, had made a tremendous effort to fly the course. It is pleasing to see how the contest always brought out the sporting instincts of the competitors.

So in 1920 the event was transferred to Venice, where Italy won. They won in 1921 as well, but were prevented from gaining the Trophy for all time in 1922 by an Englishman, H. C. Biard, who flew the course at the greatly improved rate of 145·7 m.p.h. in a Supermarine Flying Boat. But such was the financial strain that this was the last contest to be won by private enterprise. The English now had the choice again, and chose the Solent off Cowes, which was getting distinctly near home. This 1923 race was made memorable by the entry of the Americans in force. They came with a team of aircraft, craftsmen and pilots with which no private individual could hope to compete; and, of course, they won the race, at 177·38 m.p.h. Next year, the only British competitor – a Gloster Seaplane – had the misfortune to be damaged during trials; whereupon the Americans, not to be outdone in courtesy, very generously cancelled the contest for the year, instead of claiming a win as they might have done. And as things turned out, this sporting gesture kept the contest alive because in 1925 at Baltimore another American gained an easy victory with a speed of 232·57 m.p.h.

And now, when it looked as though America was going to win, Italy took up the running again and prevented the end of the contest by winning the race of 1926. Next year, back off Venice, Great Britain, represented by the R.A.F. itself, made a tremendous effort and secured the victory again, Flight-Lieutenant S. N. Webster doing 281·66 m.p.h. in a Supermarine S.5 with a Napier Lion engine. It was now agreed on all hands that one-year intervals were not enough to allow for the production of new types of aircraft and engines. So the next race did not take place until 1929. And then the venue was Spithead.

The day arrived. The course laid down was a four-sided one. The extreme easterly marker (where the turning angle was very acute) was a point in the sea due south of Hayling Island and due east of Ryde. The even sharper western corner was due north of West Cowes, and the very obtuse-angled northern and southern points were off Southsea Common and St Helens Point respectively. There were entries from three countries – the U.S.A., Italy and Great Britain – and one of the British pilots, Flying Officer H. R. D. Waghorn, R.A.F., was the victor, on a later Supermarine S.6, which flew at 328·63 m.p.h. (Note the consistent rises in speed every year when there was a contest, from 45·75 m.p.h. in 1913).

So in 1931 the venue was Spithead once more, and the holders for the moment were keyed up to win again, so that the Trophy should be theirs. And they did win again, quite comfortably. But how? It must be recalled that 1931 was a year of world economic slump, stemming from the great crisis in America of that year. Great Britain too was hit, and the R.A.F., feeling rightly or wrongly that the cost of defending the Schneider Trophy was not justified by the prestige which would accrue if we won it, refused to put up the necessary funds. Fortunately, however, there are others in this country who are not Government Departments, and in emergency they are seldom backward. And now such a one appeared on the scene, in good time too, and offered to shoulder the expense. This sporting benefactress – for it was a lady – gave £100,000 of her own money to the good cause. The name of Dame Fanny Houston should not be forgotten.

So at the post on September 13, 1931 – one day late because of bad weather – there lined up nine competitors, three each from France, Italy and Great Britain. Seven times, anti-clockwise, they flew round the triangular course[1], and the winner was Flight-Lieutenant (later Air Chief Marshall Sir) John Boothman, who averaged 340·08 m.p.h. So after eighteen hectic years of cut-and-thrust, the Trophy – and the glory – at last became ours.

Untold numbers of spectators in every known type of craft – H.M. ships, yachts, hired steamers, passing liners, merchantmen and tankers, motor boats and rowing boats – watched the race. On land every conceivable vantage point held its crowd of craning spectators. On Southsea Common there were thousands, and they stretched past Gosport to Stokes Bay, and all along the north shore of the Island from Bembridge to East Cowes. Loud-hailers blared out the times of each competitor on each lap. And doubtless everybody enjoyed himself, because this was a great day for Britain. By a sad chance, the present author was there to see the fun, yet missed it. He arrived on the north shore of the Solent on the scheduled day – September 12 – but exactly the same instant there

[1] No longer four-sided. For its exact position, see fig. 4.

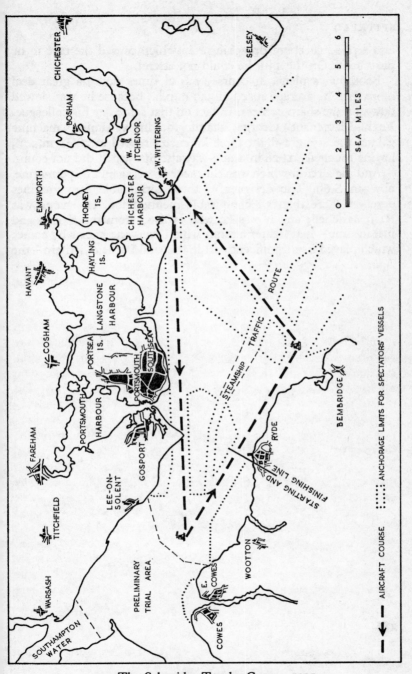

4.  The Schneider Trophy Course, 1931

also arrived sheets of drenching rain which caused the race to be postponed. On the 13th he could not attend.

Boothman's plane, of course, was at times doing a great deal more than its average speed of 340 m.p.h., because he was slowed down by the sharp corners. In fact on that same day his colleague, Flight-Lieutenant George Stainforth, in a similar machine gained the straight-flight three kilometer record at 386·1 m.p.h., having touched 404·26 in a one-way attempt which did not count.

And the aircraft which won the race? It was again a Supermarine, now an S.6b. The designer of these formidable Supermarines deserves more than an honourable mention too. His name was R. J. Mitchell; and it was he who evolved from the S.6b – and just in time – that fighter aircraft which everyone knows by name; which played its magnificent part in the vital Battle of Britain – the *Spitfire*.

## Chapter IX

# AMATEURS AFLOAT

by Robert Sutherland Horne

It has fallen to my lot to put the last chapter to the last book of Michael Lewis. It is not for me to attempt an imitation of his inimitable style, but rather, I feel, to try to pick up what would have been his subject and to treat it from the point of view of one who has lived on the shores of Spithead for nearly sixty years and sailed its waters for over fifty.

Spithead presents different faces to different people. To the holidaymaker, it is relaxation, sunshine, ever-changing scenery and sea-scapes; to the New World tourist, an old world to explore; to the sunburnt returning exile, the anticipated but still startling reminder of how green our countryside is. To the Royal Navy it means leave, refits and courses; to the navigator of large ships, an area of narrow channels beset by yachtsmen who still think that steam gives way to sail. To thousands of children, Spithead is their first sight of the sea, and its ferries are their first experience of sea-going. It is sad that the last paddle steamer has now left the Portsmouth-Ryde ferry service; one of my happiest memories is of being allowed to cross in its engine-room.

Very insular indeed were the Islanders when we lived in Wight in the nineteen-twenties, and despite the Great War, then just over, a great number of them had never been off the Island. Spithead and the Solent are their moat, their defence against the dreaded Overners – people from over the water – which is still their name for mainlanders. They would ultimately raise a Unilateral Declaration of Independence should anyone dare to propose a bridge to the Island; and who could suggest that they were not right?

When I was a boy, it was fun to move around the Island. One of the first electric tramways in the world ran down Ryde Pier, the generator being driven, as I remember it, by a slow-thudding gas engine with a huge flywheel. Later the old Victorian coaches were given diesel engines. But now the tramway is no more; nor is the old pavilion on the pier head in which we used to roller skate in the winter holidays. The little 0-4-0 locos which drew the antique coaches on the Isle of Wight Railway were changed when the Southern Railway took over. The new ones were much more modern, but still looked like museum pieces to people from the mainland. Now, alas, Beeching has caused the railway to all but vanish from the Island; it goes now only between Ryde Pierhead and Ventnor, and the ex-London Underground coaches it uses look very odd in their blue-grey livery. It was a delight, too, to drive a pony and trap through the Island's narrow lanes; a Model T Ford was the best hill-climbing motor car; and when we rode in the ex-London General Omnibus Company double-decker steam bus which ran on the Toll Road through Springvale and up the steep winding hill behind Puckpool Battery, puffing and blowing and steaming and smoking, the conductor would call out, 'All gentlemen get out and walk, please!', and all would, including this nine-year-old.

It was the motor charabanc that widened out the Island roads, but the introduction of larger car ferries at Wootton and Yarmouth loosed upon the roads an increasing congestion that swallowed up all the advantages gained. No longer dare one attempt to drive a tandem of ponies on the Island roads. The motor coaches can never take the place of old Sam Pearce, the Ryde horse dealer who used to cross to Portsmouth on the ferry, and whilst coming back over Spithead would walk the deck in his many-caped mid-nineteenth-century coachman's dress and magnificent broad red waistcoat, carrying his long whip, and collect a set of passengers for his splendid stage coach and four, which he drove on daily tours round the Isle of Wight, changing his teams at posts on the way.

The longer I live, the more I feel that the Islanders are right. Their insularity is a long-sighted virtue, improved communications are a snare and a delusion, and the internal combustion engine is the invention of the devil.

Especially as regards yachting. To me the pleasure of sailing lies much in the silence of motion and the lack of vibration. It is a lovely thing on a quiet evening to glide under sail into a half-empty creek and anchor. But nowadays this is difficult to do. Creeks on the south coast are rarely half-empty of craft, or silent. More people are sailing than ever before; almost every sailing yacht has an auxiliary; there are more motor yachts now than sailing; and outboard motors rend the silence everywhere.

Sailing craft have existed for at least six thousand years, and were used for ceremonial and sporting purposes even in antiquity. Cleopatra's Royal Yacht on the Nile was probably not the first of her kind. Of the meeting of Antony and Cleopatra, Plutarch records:

> She came in a vessel the stern whereof was gold, the sails of purple silk and the oars of silver, which gently kept time to the sound of music. She placed herself under a rich canopy of cloth of gold, habited like Venus rising from the sea, with beautiful boys about her like Cupids, fanning her; and her women representing the Nereids and Graces leant negligently on the sides and shrouds of the vessel, whilst troupes of virgins, richly dressed, marched along the banks.

In this Royal Yacht (manned only by females and small boys?) the Queen crossed the Mediterranean to Cilicia and went up the River Cydnus.

Our home waters have never perhaps seen a display of this kind. The first known royal yachtsman in the British Isles was the Scottish King Robert, who was master of his own pleasure vessel as long ago as 1326, though it was not yet known as a yacht. Yachts were in fact developed by the Dutch, who used them for 'parade sailing' in formation under orders of an 'Admiral' and firing their brass cannon in salutes. Probably the first yacht seen in England, and the first Royal Yacht proper, was the *Mary*, presented on his Restoration to Charles II by the Burgomaster of Amsterdam. The first yacht to sail Spithead – the precursor of who knows how many thousands – was probably the *Katherine*, in which Charles came on one of his many visits to Portsmouth. His brother James, ever intensely interested in nautical affairs, also became addicted to yachts, and within a couple of years brotherly rivalry had them racing in the Thames Estuary. Thus they began not only the name but also the sport of yachting, in contrast to the sedate Dutch parades. Between them they built twenty-four yachts, besides the *Mary* and *Bezan* given to Charles by the Dutch. The yachts ranged from 22 to 180 tons burden, and mostly had eight saluting guns and a crew of about thirty. The Dutch ones had lee-boards but the English were deep keel boats. One of them, the little *Fubbs*, appeared in the Navy List for ninety years, with one rebuild, and was not broken up until 1770.

The Hanoverians kept up the Royal Yachts, and Queen Victoria inherited the *Royal George*, a fine ship-rigged frigate, but times were changing. In 1842 Her Majesty left London for Leith but was held up by calms, and the *Royal George* had to be towed all the way in the reeking wake of a paddler, being overtaken by every steamer going northward. On arrival the Queen ordered the Admiralty to provide a suitable steamer to take her back, and to provide her with a steam-driven Royal Yacht for the following summer. Their Lordships had to charter a thousand-ton liner to return her to London, and Sir William Symonds, Surveyor of the Navy, designed the Royal Yacht *Windsor Castle*, which was launched the following year at Pembroke Dockyard as the *Victoria and Albert I*. In the time available it was difficult to find suitable engines, and the light weight of those fitted caused the ship to float so stern-high that it was said they dared not go ahead on her paddles lest she took a dive to the bottom. The engines were changed at vast expense and in June 1843 she berthed at Southampton to ferry the Queen to Ryde Pier. It was a filthy wet day, but Her Majesty was loyally conducted aboard by the gallant Mayor and Corporation, who stood on their pier and waved farewell, then rushed home to climb out of their robes, dripping red dye as they ran. Arriving at Ryde Pier, the mate of the yacht, in his anxiety that Her Majesty should not fall from the slippery gangway, himself fell overboard, fortunately without serious injury.

Today people are apt to think of Queen Victoria in the guise of the Widow of Windsor and 'We are not amused'. They forget that she was a venturesome young woman, who was the first Queen to own a steam yacht and probably the first woman to do so. She was very interested in cruising, and kept her fleet of yachts busy. She built no less than eight steam yachts in all, although the last of them, the *Victoria and Albert III*, a handsome screw steamer, was not completed until just after her death.

A few days before the Battle of Waterloo 'The Yacht Club' was formed at a meeting in London; in 1820 George IV gave it its warrant as 'The Royal Yacht Club' and later as 'The Royal Yacht Squadron'. They made their club-house at Cowes Castle. The presence of the Queen and Royal Family at Osborne House and the interest of the Prince of Wales (King Edward VII), added to the beauties and safe harbours of the Solent and Spithead, have made Cowes the world centre of yachting.

In the early days, yacht racing was taken no less seriously than now, but yachtsmen were perhaps more uninhibited. In the 1829 King's Cup race, Thomas Assheton Smith's *Menai*, running back from rounding the Nab, went aground on Ryde Sands, while Joseph Weld's *Lulworth* and Lord Belfast's *Louisa* ran on westward past Cowes and round the mark off Yarmouth to return to the Royal Yacht Squadron's finishing line off Cowes Castle. It was the King's birthday, and as they beat up to the line in the early darkness, all the yachts were preparing to fire their brass cannon in a Royal Salute, and the firework display was about to give the signal. The two big yachts were approaching the finishing line seconds apart and Belfast's *Louisa* had right of way when, in the excitement, *Lulworth* somehow misjudged and rammed her. All was chaos. The Royal Salute was being fired, and the fireworks were lighting up the scene of battle to reveal that, in blind fury, Belfast had ordered 'Away boarders!' and the men of the *Louisa* were swarming over the *Lulworth* with cutlasses and axes. The furious owners went racing ashore to protest to the Committee. The

Stewards ruled in favour of Belfast as having right of way, but they deemed the use of axes to cut away the rigging to be 'unjustifiable'. Only three days later *Louisa* caught *Menai* on the port tack and took advantage of it to ram her, whereupon Assheton Smith and Weld vowed never to race against Belfast again. Their quarrels spoiled a whole season's racing. Eventually his lordship triumphed. By offering ever-increasing stakes he lured Weld into a race round the Island for a thousand pounds, in which *Louisa* defeated Weld's new *Alarm*. Lord Belfast then proclaimed that he had 'proved to the world' that he owned the fastest cutter afloat, and that he intended to have the fastest square-rigger. The brig *Waterwitch* that he then built became a sore trial to the Navy. She used to lurk outside Portsmouth Harbour in wait for naval vessels leaving the port, and when they came out she would overtake them, if possible under reduced sail. In the end the Admiralty bought the *Waterwitch* as a trial horse against which to test their improved designs. So his unpopular Lordship made good his boast and won all along the line. *Waterwitch* was later to make a fortune in prize money for her captain when employed on anti-slavery patrol on the West African coast.

Assheton Smith had to resign from the Squadron in 1830 under a rule which declared anyone who should apply an engine to his yacht to be 'disqualified and ceasing to be a member'. The rule was passed at a time when he had just ordered a 400-ton steam yacht, to cost £20,000 (about £160,000 in today's currency), which was also to be named *Menai*. The adoption of steam propulsion for the *Victoria and Albert* in 1843, however, set the seal of respectability upon steam yachts.

Between 1863 and his death in 1910, as Prince of Wales and as King, Edward VII owned eight yachts, the last being the big gaff cutter *Britannia,* built on the Clyde by G. L. Watson at a total cost of £8,000. In 1897 the Prince of Wales sold her, but bought her back two years later and kept her until his death, as did his son, King George V, who was at the helm in 1930 when she won her two-hundredth victory.

The Royal Victoria Yacht Club and the temporary signal station of the Royal Thames Yacht Club on Ryde Pier were the centres of the Ryde Regatta, the main Regatta in Spithead when I was a boy, and in which the Big Class were always in full force. *Britannia's* chief rival was usually *Westward*, a great schooner owned by one of the legendary figures of yachting, T. B. Davis, a very rough diamond indeed. He was a Channel Islander who had been a stevedore at Durban, made a fortune on the Rand, and was now making a name with *Westward*. He was a hard, rough man with a stevedore's vocabulary who seldom called a spade a spade and delighted the King with his colourful phraseology. He frequently supplemented his crew by posting a notice on the wardroom noticeboard in the Royal Naval Barracks, 'R.V. Ryde Pier head 0930 hours'. Any officer not ready on the steps at 0930 to the second had to find his own way out to *Westward*. There was always an excellent buffet lunch aboard, though one seldom had any time to eat it.

On one occasion during a race, when a famous Admiral of the Fleet and his wife were T.B.'s guests, there was a sudden roar 'Ready about!', then, in the same breath, 'Tell that woman to take her bottom off the bloody sheet! Lee O!' On another occasion he borrowed for the day's racing some boys from the old clipper *Cutty Sark*, then a training ship at Falmouth. For some reason he took a dislike to one of the boys, called him a lubber and plagued him all day. The boy took it quietly and without protest; then, as they filed over the side to return to the *Cutty Sark*, the boy stepped out of line, with a single blow laid his tormentor cold upon the deck, and, still silent, went on his way. When T.B. recovered his senses he called his launch alongside and went chasing off to the *Cutty Sark* to find the boy and present him with a fiver.

King George V could be as salty as Davis himself. When asking the significance of the 'J' on the mainsail of the new Bermudan-rigged Big Class he remarked, as Heckstall-Smith relates in his most amusing book *Sacred Cowes*, 'It ought to be A Class: A for adultery, because with the exception of old Davis, I am the only owner in the class who still has his original wife!'

The peak of Davis's yachting career must have been reached one day when the Big Class were racing at Spithead and *Westward* and *Britannia* were leading them back from the Nab to the finish off the Royal Yacht Squadron at Cowes Castle. As they beat into Cowes Roads it was clear that *Westward* could not win unless she could cross the finishing line in only one more tack. To do this she must charge right in on the shallows known as the Shrape, which was thickly covered with yachts of all sizes. The dangers were that if *Westward* ran aground she might bring her great masts crashing over the side and smash and sink any craft within reach; or, should she collide with or ram another yacht, she would probably sink her or even cut her in half. Davis sent his skipper to the wheel and went to con her from up forward by hand signals. To those who watched from the shore and especially to those who watched from yachts that lay in *Westward*'s path, it looked as if disaster was inevitable as she charged through the close-packed yachts into ever-shallowing water. At the last possible moment Davis swept his arm down and roared 'Lee O!'; round she came, picked her way neatly through the moored yachts out into deeper water and swept across the finishing line just ahead of *Britannia* in one of the finest finishes ever seen.

In those days every boy on the shores of Spithead and the Solent knew the names of the big yachts racing with *Britannia* and *Westward*: the *White Heather, Cambria, Velsheda* (named after the owner's three daughters Velma, Sheila and Daphne), *Astra* (the smallest of the class) and the *Shamrocks* and *Endeavours*. I watched *Shamrock V* and the two *Endeavours* being built at Camper and Nicholson's Gosport yard, the acme of the yachtbuilder's craft.

After the 1939-45 war no one could afford to race the big yachts, nor, perhaps, would it have been advisable in the political climate of the time, a time when at the Coronation Review the Navy's firework display could only be described as cheeseparing and tawdry. The prices of yacht-building had gone up sixfold. The biggest craft now to race were the Twelve-metre Class, which were about half the size of the old J Class and were now accepted for the America's Cup race. Together with the general decrease in size of yachts came a great increase in numbers. More people than ever before took up yachting and literally hundreds more sailing clubs sprang up on the coasts and on inland waters

Nowadays the number of entries for the Round the Island Race is about four hundred, and to see this fleet coming in from the Nab Tower, running through Spithead with spinnakers set, is for me one of the finest sights in the world today; and nowhere could there be a finer setting than Spithead.

One of the causes of the astonishing boom in boating has been the Daily Express Boat Show held in London every January, when all types of yachts and dinghies are exhibited. Rarely has there been a more outstanding display of the power of publicity to sway the masses. Thousands of people become infected with a wild enthusiasm for boats of all sorts. I say 'wild enthusiasm' because it is by no means always governed by knowledge, sense or caution. One such person bought a fair-sized motor cruiser and was setting off from a South Wales port for the Solent when the Harbourmaster asked if he had the charts. 'Oh no!' he replied, 'I shan't need them. I'll be keeping close to the coast all the way round!'

A classic example was the man who came to Spithead with a brand-new speedboat and a powerful outboard engine. He launched it at Eastney, saying he was going round the Nab Tower. For some reason, after he had set off, his wife thought he had not enough petrol and raised an alarm with the Eastney Lifeboat Station. The coastguard radioed the Nab Tower, who replied that they had not seen him. The Eastney Inshore Rescue Boat of the Royal National Lifeboat Institution put out to search and eventually found the man drifting in his lifejacket, without any sign of his speedboat, miles away from where they could have been expected to find him. He was very puzzled as to what had happened. He had been roaring along when there was a thunderous crash behind, followed by comparative silence. He looked back to find the engine and after half of the speedboat had vanished. A moment later he was alone on the face of the waters. It transpired that he had set out on a course that was 70 degrees in error, mistaking the Horse and Dean Fort for the Nab Tower, crossed the barrier of concrete blocks that lay submerged between the fort and the shore, and torn the engine and stern of his boat clean off.

There has long been a lifeboat of the R.N.L.I. stationed at Bembridge, and its launches are often spectacular. First comes the sound of the maroons, then the stream of men in ordinary clothes running out along the narrow pier (just wide enough for one man) to the lifeboat house, each eager to make sure of his place in the crew by grabbing a life-jacket. The doors are opened and secured and, when all are ready, the trigger is released and the boat hurls itself down the steep ramp into the waves. About 1964 one of the early Inshore Rescue Boats was added to the complement at Bembridge, to be followed in 1965 by another at Eastney where the local auxiliary detachment of H.M. Coastguard Service were already doing very good work with unsatisfactory boats in saving life in the tricky and fast tides and shoals around the entrance to Langstone Harbour. Working in close co-operation with the adjoining coastguards, the R.N.L.I. Inshore Rescue Boat Station at Eastney has been one of the busiest in the service, and in six years has produced a remarkable record. The boats (one inflatable and one fibreglass MacLachlan boat) have been launched on service 161 times, saved 56 boats, escorted or stood by 47 boats, given help in 67 incidents, landed 52 persons and rescued 163 people. In the course of these activities nearly a dozen awards of the thanks of the Institution on vellum have been made to crew members and seven letters of commendation awarded. And other R.N.L.I. awards have been made to the Eastney Auxiliary Coastguards.

One wonders how long these voluntary services will be able to cope with the demands upon them. We have already had the spectacle of tanker collision in the Channel and a blazing tanker anchored off the Island with Inshore Rescue Boats ferrying out oxygen cylinders for exhausted firemen. Spithead was saved on that occasion by the forward planning of the naval authorities at Portsmouth, but it is a reminder that the beauties of our coast exist under constant threat.

Spithead yachting is indeed enjoying an unprecedented expansion. But its boats are not confined to purely local waters. In August 1925 a small group arranged a yacht race from Ryde Pier head along the South Coast to Land's End, round the Fastnet Rock off Ireland, and back to Plymouth, a distance of some 600 miles. It was won by a sturdy gaff cruiser, a former French pilot cutter called *Jolie Brise,* and her owner Commander Martin.

At the celebratory dinner in Plymouth, Commander Martin proposed the foundation of the Ocean Racing Club. This was done, and in 1931 it became the Royal Ocean Racing Club.

The next year *Jolie Brise*, then owned by Robert Somerville, achieved fame for a magnificent rescue in the Atlantic. She was taking part in the 600-mile New York-Bermuda Race, which is held every two years, alternating with its British counterpart the Fastnet. It was a dark and stormy night when her watch on deck became aware of lights some four miles astern, with distress signals among them. The *Jolie Brise* turned back to discover that it was a vessel on fire, and, when they got near, that it was the American yacht *Adriana*, the largest yacht in the race. Somerville determined to sail up alongside to take the crew off. *Adriana's* helmsman kept his ship steady long enough to make this possible, and *Jolie Brise* swept alongside at six knots to snatch off ten American crewmen; but before the helmsman could dodge around the flames to escape he was swept into the sea and lost in the darkness, although the *Jolie Brise* searched the area desperately in the rough seas for over an hour.

On traditions such as this the R.O.R.C. has built up a solid membership of hard, skilled seamen, entry to which is to be gained only by completing an R.O.R.C. race of more than 200 miles and by holding a certificate of competency granted by the owner or his representative.

There are a dozen or so races run by the Club each year, and many of them start from Spithead, off the Royal Albert Yacht Club's signal station on Southsea beach. The races are run in three classes by waterline length, each yacht having its own individual handicap based upon an exact formula of measurement. Crowds come to the shore to watch the starts, and a very fine spectacle it is on a breezy day, with the fleet of yachts fighting for a good start within a few yards of the spectators before tearing away across Spithead and out by the Nab Tower. Of late the presence of the Rt. Hon. Edward Heath, M.P., Prime Minister of Great Britain, appearing in the role of Ted Heath, owner and skipper of the Class I ocean racer *Morning Cloud II* and captain of the British team in the international Admiral's Cup competition, has added greatly to the number of spectators. I fear, however, that much of the interest created has been sensational and political rather than nautical. None the less, Mr Heath has the distinction of being the first British Prime Minister to become a prominent figure in yacht racing. Though the ownership and running of an ocean racer require a certain amount of wealth, the sport (which one disgruntled owner described as 'sitting in a cold shower bath tearing up £5 notes') is not one in which money alone can purchase eminence; only skill, courage and determination will do that, among men who are no respecters of persons and are as stern in their judgements as the sea they race on.

Small as are some of the R.O.R.C. craft, those of the Junior Offshore group are usually smaller, ranging from sixteen to twenty feet on the waterline. This class of diminutive but extremely sea-worthy deep-keel boats was started in 1950. They were at first regarded as too small to be safe, until Pat Ellam and Colin Moodie sailed the 16-foot *Sopranino* down to Casablanca and across via the West Indies to New York. Unfortunately the success of such enterprises by men of supreme skill all too frequently prompts men of less ability to attempt similar feats. Too many mediocre people imagine themselves to be the equals of Ellam and Moodie or of Uffa Fox, the professional boatbuilder and international racing champion. In 1928 with *Avenger*, a 14-foot international racing dinghy designed and built by himself, he won the Prince of Wales Cup by nearly five minutes, and actually lapped fourteen of his opponents. Later, with two friends and three hundredweight of gear, he sailed *Avenger* from Cowes to a regatta at Le Havre in poor weather, won all the races for which she was entered, then sailed back to Cowes with the same lading in big seas, beating all the way against a stiff breeze. He covered the hundred-mile beat to windward in thirty-seven hours: a magnificent feat, by a master. Now, alas, Uffa's doctor has had to forbid him to climb stairs but, undefeated, he has had built a bosun's chair with an electric crane to hoist him out of his riverside house at Cowes into his dinghy floating alongside.

Spithead seems to have few if any ghost stories. Indeed the only one known to me is a personal one. Three of us were sailing a half-decked boat back from Seaview to Portsmouth late one October evening, with a brisk breeze on the quarter. We were in the triangle formed by Fort Gilkicker, Southsea Castle and the Harbour mouth. It was very dark and, it being late in the year, the festoons of lights on Southsea front were no longer lit. Bob, an officer from a submarine at Fort Blockhouse, called out that he had just seen a sail across our bows making for the Harbour. After a while we found ourselves overtaking what looked like a Viking boat with only one person visible, crouched up aft steering, and with a glow on her dark squaresail as if from a lantern down below. we called out 'Good night!' but got no answer, although we were only a few yards off. We merely thought 'Unsociable blighter', and sailed on ahead. We were a good hour in the harbour entrance getting the boat up the slipway and we kept watch for the stranger. She did not come, although, with wind and tide as they were, there was nowhere else that she could go. No one we asked knew of a vessel of her description in the locality. A ghost? Who can say? If it was, it is the only ghost of Spithead that I have heard of. Not far outside, Portchester Castle has its 'well-authenticated' ghost stories, which mostly relate to the time of the Napoleonic prisoners of war; and Fort Cumberland, at the entrance to Langstone Harbour, has a ghost which even in the stern days of the Nazi war caused the Royal Marines to mount double sentries on one post in a bastion of the fort. But it is curious that in Spithead itself, with all the history that has been made there and with all the violence it has seen, the spirits lie so quiet.

# INDEX

**201**

Wight, Isle of: origin, 20, 22; name, 29; under Romans, 29, 30, 31; under Saxons, 32–3; under Danes, 36; attacked in Middle Ages, 44–7; attacked in 1545, 61; Armada fight off, 66–73; captured, 75; threatened, 77; Charles II in, 160; ferries to, 179–81, 187, 188; character of

people, 187–9; yachting, 191–8
William I, 36–7, 38; III, 76–7, 118–20, 161–2; IV, 91, 160, 166–7
Winchester, 28, 29, 30, 35
Wrotham, William de, 43

Yachts and yachting, 158, 189–99
Yarmouth, 46, 188, 191

# INDEX OF SHIPS